"Erin Lane is a writer to watch—to read with focused attention now, certainly, but also to watch. Articulate, candid beyond all caution, and cosmopolitan in experience, she is passionate about the values, stances and experiences of the millennial generation to which she belongs. The result is one of the clearest and certainly one of the most informing pictures I have seen to date of the generation of young adults who presently are shaping the twenty-first-century church."
Phyllis Tickle, author of *The Great Emergence*

"This is the kind of book I'd like to hand to millennials and church leaders, and say, 'Read this!' As Lane shares her 'commitment phobe' story, she is charitable, vulnerable and full of conviction about how we are all to be the church and about how we are all to belong to one another. I admire her charity toward and communion with believers and congregations who hold different convictions than she does. Oh, that we too would model her charity and engagement!"
Marlena Graves, author of *A Beautiful Disaster: Finding Hope in the Midst of Brokenness*

"Like Erin, I'm a bit of a commitment phobe myself, and moving more than five times in my first decade of full-fledged adulthood (like many of my generation) hasn't helped. Through her theological and personal storytelling in this eloquently crafted book, Lane offers those who are weary and cynical a glimpse at—and an invitation to—discovering the imperfect wonder of life together in Christ."
Rachel Marie Stone, author of *Eat with Joy*

"Erin Lane holds out here an inescapable enigma: we are both singular and communal beings. In passion, humor, angst and eccentricity, she gives us windows into her particular story. But, but, but, she does so as she takes us with her on a meandering, start and stop, disappointing and yearning journey to find Christian community. Like her, we long for what is genuine and intimate but not coercive, invasive or smarmy—in other words, we long for what is very hard to find. Erin is a candid, pained and hilarious guide who illustrates what makes community so rich but so elusive. She portrays the challenges, admits and tempers the tensions, and reassures us of the grace and beauty of what is possible, even if it is inevitably partial."
Mark Labberton, president, Fuller Theological Seminary, author of *Called*

D1469076

"The church's thinkers have rightly turned toward community, but real community is difficult before it is life-saving. This book disillusions us from community-in-dreams to return us to the ordinary, everyday body of Christ. The church is a headache, and it is worthy of our longing for it. This book is wise, tender, patient and beautiful."

Jason Byassee, author of *Discerning the Body*

"Erin Lane skillfully weaves insights about marriage and the church, God and anthropology, physics and spirituality, into a thoroughly engaging personal narrative that is a great pleasure to read. *Lessons in Belonging* is funny, smart and full of wisdom from a wide array of sources—Einstein, ancient tradition, Lane's acquaintances and friends. It may convince you—in these days of increasing privatization and insulation—that going to church is a beautiful and important countercultural move. Or it may simply charm you with its lively stories and intriguing cast of characters. It's a wonderful book however you approach it."

Debbie Blue, author of *Consider the Birds*, founding minister, House of Mercy Church, St. Paul

"Plenty of folks want Jesus but not the church. . . . In this raw, winsome book, Erin cuts through the fluff. She has seen the funk of Christianity—but she has fallen in love with a beautiful God whose grace overshadows the funk of the church. She reminds us that the church is not a meeting or a building, not something you go to—the church is something we are, a living body, a community where imperfect people can fall in love with a perfect God and hopefully help each other become a little better. Erin reminds us that the real question isn't whether or not Christians are hypocrites, but whether we can be honest enough to make room for another hypocrite among us. It's a lovely book for folks who love the church, and folks who want to but aren't there yet."

Shane Claiborne, author of *The Irresistible Revolution*

"Erin Lane has written a compelling, candid narrative—a testimony—with lessons for all of us about belonging and longing. Read it to learn from a millennial about the perennial desire of the human heart to connect and how a life with God can meet those needs. Wonderful. Practical. Theology."

The Rev. Jacqueline J. Lewis, Middle Collegiate Church

LESSONS IN BELONGING

FROM A CHURCH-GOING COMMITMENT PHOBE

ERIN S. LANE

FOREWORD BY PARKER J. PALMER

IVP Books

An imprint of InterVarsity Press
Downers Grove, Illinois

InterVarsity Press
P.O. Box 1400, Downers Grove, IL 60515-1426
ivpress.com
email@ivpress.com

InterVarsity Press® is the book-publishing division of InterVarsity Christian Fellowship/USA®, a movement of students and faculty active on campus at hundreds of universities, colleges and schools of nursing in the United States of America, and a member movement of the International Fellowship of Evangelical Students. For information about local and regional activities, visit intervarsity.org.

Scripture quotations, unless otherwise noted, are from the New Revised Standard Version of the Bible, copyright 1989 by the Division of Christian Education of the National Council of the Churches of Christ in the USA. Used by permission. All rights reserved.

While the stories in this book are based on real people and events, some names and identifying information may have been changed to protect the privacy of individuals.

Cover design: Cindy Kiple
Interior design: Beth McGill

Images: ©Zoran Zeremski/iStockphoto

ISBN 978-0-8308-4317-6 (print)
ISBN 978-0-8308-9762-9 (digital)

Printed in the United States of America ∞

Library of Congress Cataloging-in-Publication Data

Lane, Erin, 1984–
  Lessons in belonging from a church-going commitment phobe / Erin S.
Lane ; foreword by Parker J. Palmer.
    pages cm
  Includes bibliographical references.
  ISBN 978-0-8308-4317-6 (pbk. : alk. paper)
  1. Church. 2. Belonging (Social psychology) I. Title.
  BV600.3.L36 2015
  250—dc23

                                                    2014035586

P   21   20   19   18   17   16   15   14   13   12   11   10   9   8   7   6   5   4   3   2   1

Y   33   32   31   30   29   28   27   26   25   24   23   22   21   20   19   18   17   16   15

This book is dedicated to my family,

the seedbed of my belonging and the source of my walking roots.

I picture us like the mangrove trees propping ourselves up

against the tides and sipping oxygen like straws.

We may look anemic, but we are survivors.

To Perk,

who taught me how to trust my whims

as whispers of the Spirit

To Dad,

who taught me how to show up

past the point of comfort

To Charlie,

who taught me that to go big you

have to risk it all sometimes

To Rush,

my plot of solid ground.

Your stability allows me to soar.

CONTENTS

FOREWORD

At age seventy-five, I'm a very lucky guy. As a writer, teacher and activist who seems to lack retirement skills, I have regular opportunities to work with insightful, engaged and engaging people half my age or less. They're important to me not only because of their life-giving spirits, but also as my distant early warning system.

At my age, I feel as if I'm standing somewhere down the curvature of the earth, no longer able to see the horizon that the young can see from where they stand, higher up that curve. To be alive and responsive to the world as it is today, I need younger people to tell me what they see and hear coming across that horizon, because it's coming my way too. (Note for older readers: the phrase "I'm standing somewhere down the curvature of the earth" is a clever way of saying I'm over the hill without making it sound too bad.)

Erin Lane, who wrote this book in her late twenties, is a friend and valued colleague at the Center for Courage & Renewal, a nonprofit I founded some twenty years ago. As this important book reveals, she is passionately engaged with what it means to "be church" and with calling the church to its fullest potential. Even more fundamentally, she is passionately engaged with what it means to be fully human—which, in my mind, means to live into the image of God in which we were all created.

If the church cannot encourage and support us in our full humanity, it does not have a future, nor does it deserve one. But what's refreshingly radical about this book is that the author spends little time berating the institutional church and its leaders for failing to address the needs of the rising generation, nearly one-third of whom don't belong to a religious organization. Instead, she locates the problem—and the solution—in the psyches of her own generation. Among Millennials, she says, "belonging is a lost art. It's not simply that we've chosen not to belong. It's that we've forgotten how."

Now that, it seems to me, is a genuine insight, worth pondering at length. And from where I stand on the earth's curvature, it applies not only to Erin Lane's generation, but to those of her parents and grandparents. This book gives all of us a new way to look at the oft-noted and oft-bemoaned decline of community and rise of individualism in our culture.

"Belonging is a lost art" up and down the generational continuum and all of us, no matter what our age, need the "lessons in belonging" that this book's title promises. It's a promise richly fulfilled time and time again as the book moves along, as this brief overview of some of its themes suggests.

- Belonging to one another is our birthright gift.

- Belonging is not a set of feelings we depend on but a set of practices we enact.

- Belonging requires a choice to trust others and risk the consequences.

- When we risk trust, we risk vulnerability, which is what ultimately deepens our belonging.

- Belonging requires discernment about which relationships and which communities can help us be and see ourselves rightly.

- Belonging gives us what we yearn for—an exchange of gifts that brings reconciliation.

That's a list of "teasers," not "spoilers," because each of these items opens big and challenging questions: How do we learn this? How do we do this? How do we stay with this, even when the going gets rough? Erin Lane never offers glib answers. In fact, she does not offer "answers" at all, and that's a good thing when the questions involved are not conventionally answerable. Instead, she offers honest, grounded, human-scale pointers to the way forward, always rooted in her own real struggle to belong.

It's Erin Lane's struggle as much as her counsel that makes this book so important. She does not preach from on high in these pages. Instead she shares her mind and heart from the trenches of what she calls "the messy business of belonging to one another." If you are looking for yet another sanitized treatise on the joys of Jesus and his church, do not open this book. But if you want real talk about real dilemmas in our own broken lives and the broken life of the church, this book is for you.

For me, one of the virtues of many Millennials is that they talk about real-life stuff with a vulnerability unknown in my generation, or those that preceded mine. If I'd heard more real-life talk when I was young, real life might not have taken me by such surprise! Erin's account of her own struggle as a "church-going commitment phobe" reminds me of the chorus of Leonard Cohen's song "Anthem": "Ring the bells that still can ring/Forget your perfect offering/There's a crack in everything/That's how the light gets in." There's a lot of light in this book.

Like most of us, I belong to a variety of communities: family, clusters of friends and colleagues, a religious community, a civic community. But unlike most people, I spent eleven years living in a so-called intentional community, where I shared a daily round of worship, work, study, social action, decision-making and common meals with some eighty people. At the end of my first year, I came up with Palmer's Definition of Community: "Community is that place where the person you least want to live with always lives." At the end of my second year, I came up with Palmer's Corollary to Palmer's Definition: "And when that person moves away, someone else arises immediately to take his or her place."

What Erin Lane understands is that the demands and vexations of life together are not the death knell of community—they are doorways into deeper relationship as we work through our disillusionments with community, others and ourselves, and find the solid ground of reality that lies beneath illusion. If more and more people could understand that fact—and hang in with one another long enough to experience the blessing—we and all the communities we belong to would be the richer for it.

This lively, insightful and beautifully written book offers the "lessons in belonging" we all need to strengthen our communities and their contributions to the world.

Parker J. Palmer

Preface

THE GIFT OF DISILLUSIONMENT

If we have no peace, it is because we have forgotten we belong to each other.

MOTHER TERESA

Each year, my college roommate Jacki comes to North Carolina for a visit. I never know when it's going to be or how she's going to get here. Neither one of us is keen on trading updates over the phone. It was New Year's Eve the last time she came. She was on her way to an Avett Brothers concert and could only stay for a day. We made the most of it by weaving in and out of thrift stores around town, touching clothes and telling stories that would have to sustain us another year. On our way home, walking tandem over narrow sidewalks, she recounted a story that has stuck with me ever since.

It was a story from an old book about a woman who took a hammer to her new car.[1] That's right. She took a hammer to her own car. I imagined it sitting in the driveway as she approached. Maybe her husband stood looking on. Or maybe he couldn't bear to watch, the weight of every penny spent felt in his gut. Either way, the outcome was the same. Her hammer met the steel frame and it buckled beneath the force. You might be confused by this surprising move. You might think she was acting out some Carrie Underwood revenge fantasy. But her action made perfect sense to me as Jacki explained it. Hitting the brand-new car with a hammer released the woman and her husband from worrying over that first ding. There would be no anxiety when parking the car next to some beat-up truck—no ambition for resale or getting their money's worth. There was only the hope that this dented body could carry them where they needed to go and the acceptance that it was theirs to tend.

Yes, I thought to myself, *this sounds right.* This is how I imagine the church. A vehicle of disillusionment.

≡ ≡ ≡

In American vernacular, we often describe disillusionment as something bad. When we say we are disillusioned by the church, we typically mean that the institution has not lived up to our expectations. It has failed us, even deceived us. While the cloak was once pulled over our eyes, now we have seen too much; too much ego in our leaders or fear in our pews or cowardice in our governing bodies. We cannot abide what is evidently true: the church is as screwed up as any institution we know—sometimes, terrifyingly, more so.

But actual disillusionment is a good thing. To be disillusioned simply means to be freed from our illusions. Looked at this way, the church should be in the business of disillusionment! The church, as I understand it, is anywhere we regularly gather to receive communion from God and practice communion with one another. It's where we go to get our reality check about who we are and to whom we belong. Surely, we need help in weeding out the lies that choke our life—lies like the illusion of alienation, that we are incapable of relationship, or the illusion of difference, that we have nothing in common with folks who believe with a faith we call blind. There's the illusion of control, that we can protect ourselves from the suffering we fear, and the illusion of separateness, that we can thrive apart from a shared community of practice. Or how about the illusion of scarcity, that our worth comes from the things we do or the things we are not—that we're not good enough until we try a little harder, become more articulate and less unsure, more faithful and less needy. Are these not the lies that keep us from living in reality? In what kind of God do we believe if that God is not the realest of the most real, the truest of the most true, the farthest thing from an illusion to which one can cling?

Disillusionment may be good, but it's never easy. Many of us have grown comfortable with our illusions. The loss of their familiar silhouette can be scary, like a night-light gone dark. Quaker author and activist Parker Palmer calls this the pain of disillusionment. "God is the great iconoclast," Palmer writes, "constantly smashing the idols on which we depend. Beyond illusion lies a fuller truth that can be glimpsed only as our falsehoods die. As we have the faith to live fully in the midst of these painful contradictions, we will experience resurrection and the transformation of our lives."[2]

Disillusionment, it turns out, is the gift of the cross. Disillusionment sets us free. But free to do what?

⊟ ⊟ ⊟

Lessons in Belonging from a Church-Going Commitment Phobe is a book for people who like the idea of church but feel disillusioned by the reality of the people who make it up. For every sermon we hear, we can think of two more that would have been more nuanced. If we can convince ourselves to endure a small group study, we are prone to answering every question with one of our own. For every impoverished song we hear in worship, for every "prayers of the people" gone rogue, for every bulletin misspelled, we wonder why exactly we're winnowing time away with people who so obviously don't get it or get us. Many of us are such fierce lovers of tradition that we're likely to grab the church by the jaw and say with mouths close, "You were meant for more than this." But I think we were meant for more than this too. I think we were made free to live like we belong to the household of God.[3]

As evidenced by the growing population of religious "nones," belonging to the church and other worshiping bodies has become a lost art, especially among my millennial generation (roughly those born between 1982 and 2004). According to surveys that were released as I prepared to write this book:

- Of all adults 18 and over, 20% are considered "nones"; that is, they are unaffiliated with any particular religion (up almost 5% from 2007 to 2012). While nearly 6% of this group describe themselves as atheists or agnostics, the remaining 14% don't use any label.[4]

- Among Americans ages 18 to 29, the percentage of those unaffiliated with a particular religion increased to a whopping 32% in one poll[5] and 27% in another, although some predict those numbers are leveling off.[6]

- Interestingly, most religiously unaffiliated Americans think that churches and other religious institutions offer some benefit to society by strengthening communities and serving the poor. But they aren't looking to be a part of them.[7]

With an ever-growing number of young people choosing not to identify themselves with a particular religion, I wrote this book to remember for myself how it is that I, a church-going commitment phobe, continue to practice belonging. There is a vast middle ground between the hyperreligious, who sometimes belong without questioning, and the nonreligious, who often question without belonging. I suggest that there is middle ground to be found and call this "faithful rebellion." It signifies the desire of many people to belong to communities of faith while "living the contradictions," as Palmer puts it.[8] Doubt is popular. Certainty is popular. Living in the in-between is messy, and often painful.

This book is not a defense for faith in God, Scripture or the tradition of the church; it is an invitation for those who believe to risk greater trust and find deeper peace in each other. Mine is a story of trying to belong to the church, to my husband, friends and strangers, too. It's a story about enduring community when it's awkward, when small talk suffocates and the preacher gives bad sermons and the suffering of others is intrusive. It's about choosing to trust people, not because they've earned it but because you want to. It's about losing yourself to other people and asking for help when you need finding again. It's about not waiting for the pastor's permission or the right conditions before you can say, "These are my gifts. I think they could be worth something here."

This is a story about failure, too.

Lessons in Belonging is not meant be a rebuttal to those who have found their identity outside of the church but instead a plea for those who can and are called to commit to the messy business of belonging to one another.

⊟ ⊟ ⊟

Belonging is a big word, and to be honest, I don't much like big words. Like brains preserved in jars of formalin and alcohol, they're too murky to have anything to do with real life. I can't understand the concept of belonging apart from the actual people I belong to on a daily basis, people like my husband, Rush. That's why there are stories in this book about how I told him he had bad breath when we first met and why I still don't trust him to call the cable company without a few "talking points." If we are to take seriously the apostle Paul's assertion that marriage is a mystery that points to the relationship between Christ and the church (Ephesians 5:32), then surely figuring out how to commit to Rush day in and day out can give me a clue as to how to commit to putting on my pants every Sunday for worship. This doesn't mean that one can't understand belonging to the church without becoming one flesh with a marriage partner. We share the flesh of belonging with our mothers in the womb, friends curled on couches and strangers on whom we lay hands. Rather, I suggest that Rush has taught me as much about my limits in community as my dog, Amelia, has taught me about my limits as a parent. I've gathered from both that I could work on my tone.

I have structured the book in six sections. Each section suggests a lesson for participating in the life of the church that was helpful to me in shedding the illusions of how belonging *should* happen and revealing the reality of how belonging *actually* happens. I think of these phenomena as the anthropology of belonging; using the experience of my first year attending a new church, I've uncovered the rituals of belonging in a particular iteration of mainline, evangelical, American Protestantism. Although my experiences are unique to me as a woman, a white person, an introvert, a Midwesterner and a millennial, I hope to offer some insight into broader patterns of belonging: why it happens, when it doesn't and what it tells us about the God who has the audacity to call us "my people."

Finally, I am grateful to my buddy Jonathan, who pointed out to me that too many Christian books read like sermonettes rather than stories. It's my intention that this book read like a hybrid of both. To this end, each section contains an explanation of the sociological or theological research behind the particular lesson or practice of church life I am describing. I hope this doesn't take the reader out of the narrative altogether but serves as a quick stop along the way for those with an appetite for something more explicit.

Parker Palmer, to whom I'm indebted for his thoughts on disillusionment and, more importantly, his generous friendship, wrote, "I've never written on a topic that I've mastered or figured out. . . . I write about things whose mystery seems bottomless to me."[9] Belonging and longing. Reality and illusion. Christ and the church. I trust these are wily enough companions to fill a lifetime's worth of writing.

And rewriting.

Lesson One

THE IMPORTANCE OF
BEING EARNEST

All I ever wanted was to belong,
to wear that hat of belonging.

ANNE LAMOTT

≡ **1** ≡

"The thing I am most desperate to keep you from finding out about
me is . . ."

I am sitting in a minimum-security women's prison, tapping my
pencil on the folding table beneath my elbows. The fluorescent lights
overhead make it hard to think without wanting to rub your eyes or
relax into a yawn. Outside it's the kind of late winter night that could
slap you awake with one blow. Inside it's warm, a put-you-to-sleep
kind of warm, warm the color of beige. There are beige paper towels
in the restroom we share, a beige utility cart that props up the television we watch and beige tables set up in a circle for writing class.
The only thing in the room that isn't beige is the milky green uniform
worn by all inmates—some in oversized T-shirts and elastic-waist
pants, others in a style that hits at the knees, like the nightgowns I
used to wear as a young girl.

I look around the room, my eyes stopping briefly on each of my
classmates before I steady my gaze on the blank page below me. When
Chaplain Kay had asked a few months back why I was here, I responded, "To live a better story." I don't think she was amused. Others
had been more direct.

For the last year and a half of my life, I've been talking to dead
people: disciples, martyrs and theologians who show up in the foot-
notes of double-spaced papers typed for graduate school. When I
began the program at age twenty-six, I had four years of "being a real,
live adult" behind me, two of which had landed me at a publishing
house in San Francisco. There I flourished press releases with adjec-
tives like "vital," "inspiring," even "peachy," in an effort to pitch religion
books to the media. If the actual work itself wasn't all those things, the
idea of it was. Once, in an introductory theology course, I tried spicing
up a writing assignment with what we in the publishing business call

a "hook," the kind of introductory sentence that sinks into your jaw and anchors your attention, when a tutor told me, "No one needs to be hooked, dear. Your preceptors are getting paid to read." Being back in the classroom might have been a "luxury" as I took to describing it, but it was fast becoming a luxury in the ancient Greek sense of the word: loosened, sluggish and out of joint with reality. A spiritual autobiography course in the local prison promised to give me new material, if for no other reason than I would have to leave the white-stained walls of the classroom to find it.

The course was being offered in partnership with Project TURN, a local program in Durham that educates persons who are incarcerated alongside those who aren't. There was something about the idea of being with the "other" among us—the modern untouchables who are often deemed unworthy of basic rights like voting, housing and fulfilling work upon release—something about the value of feeling ourselves "out of place" in order to see our own place with wider eyes. There may have also been something about reading an Anne Lamott memoir instead of another pillar of Christian doctrine named John.

"One of your incarcerated classmates has been on death row," Chaplain Kay explained to a roomful of mild-mannered students at orientation. Her short brown hair was flattened behind one ear with a bobby pin, revealing a face with an intensity that unnerved me. "And many more have ended up in prison as a result of their own experiences of abuse." We were to make space for their stories as we learned to tell our own.

Six weeks into class, I've already written about my earliest memory of God, sitting on my parents' four-post bed. It was where I learned about Jesus and, later, the divorce. I wrote, too, about the history of my last name and how I once gave it away only to beg for it back four years later. In another exercise, I admitted I was bent to know God loves everyone the same.

Then there were the stories my classmates told, of macaroni art scattered across the floor, of blood traveling up the esophagus, of the house burning down and the tears rolling hot. We swallowed the questions we were too timid to ask, Do you mean? Did you really? Do you know that wasn't your fault?

All this literary emoting was rubbing me bare.

And so I stall now answering the writing prompt, stubborn at the thought of peeling off one more layer of thick skin. I scribble something about how I still pick my nose and eat the crusties. But no, that's too easy, I think, and maybe even a little charming in that "I'm a gal who can house a pizza and pee in the woods" sort of way. Besides, this admission feels trivial in comparison to what I imagine is being pressed into the pages beside me.

My eyes flash across the room to Doris, a white woman with a Dorothy Hamill bob circa the 1976 Olympics. She is writing without much expression. I wonder, is it she who has been close to death at the hands of a broken judicial system? Or was it the hands of a broken partner? What part of herself will she allow us to witness, and what part is she desperate to bury? I want Doris to feel safe in this space; I want that for myself, too.

I know the story I have crafted for myself already. It's the one where I play the perpetual contrarian. I claim my Catholicism in a room full of Protestants, get downright evangelistic around my tribe of feminists, and can be religious, spiritual or a plain old "lover of God and people" depending on who's asking and what I think they're trying to prove. It's a story of a commitment phobe who never wanted to marry young or stay put for long. The concept of a church home feels as fleeting to me as that of a stable family.

I ready my pencil and try again. It takes a few sentences to figure out what I am trying to say once I start, but when Chaplain Kay says, "Finish your last thought," I can see the string of words pulsing off the page.

I am embarrassed just reading them.

"The thing I am most desperate to keep you from finding out about me is . . . I want to belong, but I don't know how."

I want to believe it wasn't always this way, that I wasn't always inept at the basic skill of belonging. (I also want to stop saying awkward things to people like "I'm writing a book about being awkward.") But adults have a way of becoming calloused to truths we once knew well.

When I was eleven, I noticed a patch of scratchy skin beginning to form on my upper arm. I tried to rub it off in the shower like flakes off a sunburn, but it persisted. It wasn't scaly by the time I went to the doctor for a biopsy. Like a snake, it had shed its scaly exterior and revealed a smooth, leathery patch that slithered beneath my freckles. Tests revealed it was the autoimmune disease scleroderma, a word from the Greek meaning "hard skin." Even if we treated it, it could kill me. I relished the thought of having a life-threatening disease as if it validated the drama I experienced as an adolescent trying to make a home in my ever-changing skin. They were life threatening, too, those delicate social dances that taught us who and what to belong to. If we weren't careful, we would lose the suppleness of our youthful hearts, right along with our doughy cheeks and rounded bellies.

Middle-schoolers live close to the nerve of belonging. They can name its pain and pulses clearly. When popular research professor Brené Brown interviewed a bunch of eighth graders about their definition of the word, they offered this distinction: Fitting in means I have to be like you. Belonging means I get to be me.[1] Did you catch that little word "get"? To "get" to be ourselves means that belonging is both a gift we receive and a pilgrimage we make. To be our authentic selves requires some *getting to*, some *working out*, some *travelling toward* as we discern the "me" we get to be. Learning to belong is lifetime work.

To be clear, we need help arriving as ourselves in this world. Belonging isn't just about being alone in a room with the door closed and the stereo on, with nothing but a Celine Dion song for company. Belonging is about discerning ourselves in the context of a community, a web of relationships both horizontal and vertical that gives us meaning and purpose and identity. Brown describes her own definition of belonging as "the innate human desire to be part of something larger than us."[2] For some people this something larger could be participating in a home-brew club where you come out of your hopped-up broom closet once a month to swap science and stories. For others this something larger goes beyond human community to belief in a spiritual community or a higher power as those in recovery groups like Alcoholics Anonymous are keen on calling it. For Christians, we often expect to find the source of our belonging in the church, a microcosm of the living, breathing body of God on earth.

So it's all the more tragic when the church becomes the source not of our belonging but our disappointment, a microcosm of petty, human organisms. Nowadays I hear less about how the church is a petri dish for growing connection and more about how its culture is preventing people from developing healthy relationships with God, themselves and others. Marcus Mumford, the twenty-something front man of Mumford and Sons, admitted in *Rolling Stone* that despite having personal views about the person of Jesus, "I've kind of separated myself from the culture of Christianity."[3] He's not alone. Many of us strain to see how this kind of human community can resemble the holy communion Jesus offered when he said "Take, eat; this is my body." It's no wonder that so many of us make up the growing population of religious "nones."

The nones, those folks who don't identify with any religious tradition but the majority of whom still believe in God. The nones, who think organized religion is obsessed with money, sex and rules. The nones, who at last count make up almost a third of my under-thirty peers.

I am not a none.

I am a twenty-nine-year-old who wears skinny jeans, man boots and Mac's Red Russian lipstick. I live in North Carolina but was born in Nashville, reared in Ohio, raised near Chicago, schooled in Ann Arbor, married outside of Charlotte and awakened in San Francisco. I want to live in Seattle some day, but these days I'm making my home in Durham. I call myself a Christian, and a feminist too.

I believe in being *the* church. I believe in attending *a* church. I just don't like to do it. I don't like when the older people talk too long even though I need to be reminded of our shared history. I don't like it when the young babies cry too loudly even though I need to be reminded of our shared need. I don't take well to authority figures telling *me* what to do. And yet I have a lot of opinions on what *they* should do.

I like Jesus; I just don't like when he's separated from the other persons of the Trinity like the cheese who stands alone. I believe in tradition if there's a good reason behind it. It's just that I often can't get a straight answer about what that reason is.

I have a master's degree in theology, but I don't want to hear your dissertation. I want the specifics, like how you picture God when you pray and what you say to the beggar on the street who asks for money. I am interested in women and men who want to belong and are ready to do so with people who don't look and think and act like them.

The trouble is I have a hard time committing to these people, because as pastor Lillian Daniel puts it, "In church, in community, humanity is just way too close to look good."[4]

≡ ≡ ≡

Let me be upfront. The word *commitment* is about as attractive to me as the word *submission* or *accountability*. If a friend wants to schedule a coffee date more than two weeks out, I'm prone to write back, "Let's check in then and see how we're feeling." I don't buy two of anything—perfume, deodorant, canned soup—until I'm out of the first and can be sure I'm still in the mood for another. I even refuse to record addresses in my contact book with anything but pencil. (How am I supposed to know how long this relationship will last or whether you'll update me next time you move or if I'll even want to include you on the Christmas card I keep meaning to send out?) Commitment means what was once a romantic possibility is now a real thing, with real flaws I couldn't have predicted, and worse, I can't avoid.

This is all to say that no one was more surprised than I was when, a year after writing those ten, simple words in a women's prison, I found myself at a local church considering, of all things, commitment.

I arrived on a Sunday evening, the second bike trip to church of the day, with my helmet under my arm and leather gloves tucked into my pockets. It was winter in North Carolina, and every ounce of color had gone underground. Even my wardrobe had morphed from an array of poppy flowers and navy stripes to a tired-looking fleece that appeared to be sprouting hair. I wiped snot onto my sleeve as I made my way past the staff offices and to the church parlor. The new members' class was called "The Inquirers," and I wondered if they'd be passing out capes along with our easy-peel name tags.

I took my seat at the edge of a fabric-covered couch near Martin, the senior pastor. On the other side of us was Jenny, a young Asian woman who'd been baptized at a nearby lake last summer and was moving along swiftly in her devotion. Across from us on the chair with the swirly, wooden back was Avery, a divinity school student from Palo Alto who I'd met a few times at young adult gatherings and took to admiring, although how one ventured to join a church less than six months after arriving stumped me. I chalked it up to the overachieving impulse of young women. To my right was a middle-aged couple who spoke to one another in the hushed tones of a library voice, a young couple who dropped their kids off in the nursery before arriving rumpled, and a boisterous man who was planning a wedding and liked to talk about it. But the chattiest Inquirers of all were Ralph and Marie, who had recently moved from Omaha to be near the grandkids. Marie took one look around the room when she walked in and jabbed Ralph, "Did we just stumble into the nursery?" I ventured she thought this was a compliment in a room where the median age was a disconcerting thirty. The rest of the room unfolded in polite laughter.

We went around the circle to start, introducing ourselves by sharing our favorite dessert. *I could skip the icebreakers,* I thought, even though I got really animated talking about cupcakes and how I used to think the magic was in the frosting but these days I was finding more finesse in the cake. What I really wanted to know is why they were all here, not just how long they had been here but why they were as crazy as I to consider joining a church—a church declining, some say dying. On life support even. Martin told us that within the Presbyterian denomination to which this church belongs, most congregations see more funerals than baptisms these days. Membership is at an all-time low, too, one hundred thousand less than just a year ago.[5]

So what I really want to ask you, and everyone else who had the gall to sit with me in that parlor, is *Why commit to a church at all?* Because it's what your parents did or your professors want? Or because you think it's the right example to set for your children now that they're old enough to repeat swear words in the back seat of the car? Are you really getting anything out of this, and are we even allowed to ask that? Does it matter that I don't agree with everything you do or the pastor believes or the Bible says, and how much agreement do we really need to function as a church, and if you don't mind my asking one more question, what *is* our function as a church and what's the function of a class or a covenant or a pledge to make known a membership that seems to change so very little? What I want to ask most is whether commitment is as hard for you as it is for me. If so, thank God, and if not, thank God, too, because we need all kinds of kinds here.

The truth is we are not the superheroes we'd like to be. But maybe here we can be something better than superheroes. Maybe church is where we get to be the people we really are.

ᗗ ᗗ ᗗ

I was fascinated by my scleroderma growing up. I would cross my arms in front of my chest and squeeze my left arm with my right hand and my right arm with the left for comparison. The healthy arm could be pressed into pinchable folds of skin, but the other arm would not budge, instead moving as one hard mass. First it was only a few inches long. Then it was ten. The only solution was to rub a steroid cream over the arm each day. It gave my skin a whitish sheen for the next few years, which drew attention during volleyball matches and pool parties, but I slathered it on religiously no matter how uncool it made me feel. Like religion, it reminded me that without daily attention I risked becoming hard to myself and the world.

Faced with the statistics about my generation's mistrust of organized religion, I feel lonely at the prospect of belonging to the church without them. Where will my peers be when I show up for worship and need to see myself in the crowd? Where will they be when I want to sing along to those nineties Christian rock anthems with arms outstretched? Where will they be when I'm too shy to stick around for Sunday brunch and need a gentle invitation?

It's earnestness I'm after these days. It's what I notice in other people, and it's what I'm trying to practice myself. Throughout Scripture, the Greek words translated as "earnest" are found paired with concepts like expectation (Romans 8:19; Philippians 1:20), longing (2 Corinthians 7:7, 11), and the down payment of the Spirit (2 Corinthians 1:22; 5:5; Ephesians 1:14). People who are earnest aren't afraid to name what they want even if it undoes them to say so. They aren't afraid to get their hopes up for realities yet unseen or even imagined. In fact, they're fixated on ideas such as these.[6] Some trans-

lations of the Bible even describe their waiting as "anxious" (e.g.,
Romans 8:19 NASB, Darby), which is the closest I've ever come to
finding biblical justification for my neuroses.

Sometimes I think I'm drawn to earnestness of late for the same
reason hipsters are drawn to fanny packs—it's so uncool, it's cool. With
all the throwbacks to our youth, so prevalent today in movies, music and
fashion, you'd think we'd be better at recapturing some of the zeal of
days spent playing baseball in the cul-de-sac with a tennis ball and
plastic bat, jellies substituting for tennis shoes and perms masquerading
as human hair. We care too much now about looking foolish. We care
that our Christianity comes across as informed, but a bit irreverent. God
forbid someone thinks we're a rule follower. God forbid someone thinks
we've settled. And perhaps most frightening of all, God forbid someone
thinks we could join an institution that asks us to die to ourselves when
we're still trying to find ourselves. I mean really, our prefrontal cortex—
the area of the brain that helps us make good decisions—isn't even
completely formed until our midtwenties.

I personally love the stories in Scripture where people are accused
of being drunk. It's a kind of foolishness one has to embrace to believe
that the church can be a miraculous place in which every person, tribe
and nation belong. Maybe even more miraculous is the idea that the
church can be a place where you and I belong. It seems an impossible
idea, but there it is in the long arc of our people's history: in the pages
of the prophet Isaiah, who imagines God's house perched on the top
of a mountain for all nations to gather round; in the teachings of Jesus,
who instructs his followers to be widely indiscriminate in their bap-
tizing of all peoples; and in a cacophony of languages that are somehow
understood by all on that bewildering day of Pentecost when a few
reasonable folks surmised that everyone had to be three sheets to the
wind, because you'd have to be drunk to believe such a vision of the
church is possible. You'd have to be drunk to think you'd ever belong
to that congregant who refers to "*the* gays" or your sister-in-law who

has faith only in "the energy beneath the floorboards." But wouldn't it be great if this were true? Wouldn't it be great if we got to participate in cocreating this kind of Spirit-filled, holy-fied reality?

Belonging is hard. It begs commitment and compromise and even, yes, sometimes conformity. I know, I know, I'd be tempted to put the book down here, too. But these are the things we must do if we want to grow in our faith. Paul says that such unity helps us to become mature and attain "the fullness of Christ" (Ephesians 4:12-13 NASB). Maturity and unity are inseparable as we experience communion not just with Christ but with one another. Learning to belong to the body of Christ isn't just an exercise of the shoulds; it's the mark of a Christian who is no longer driven by setting herself apart from *those* people and is instead ready to build up the church of *my* people.

Of course, first, I had to find my people.

There was something different about our move to North Carolina than the other three we'd made as husband and wife. It had the smell of permanence, like our musty guest bedroom furniture brought out of storage. We would be closer again to family. We would be within driving distance to friends' weddings. We would have a mortgage.

The heat fell heavy on my chest the first day Rush and I pulled up to the teal, twin-peaked house on Oakland Avenue. It was 110 degrees outside. Sweat pooled on my cheeks. The pink of my skin turned red with a colony of mosquito bites and an uneven sunburn. At night we stepped over the cardboard boxes that covered our bedroom floor and crawled on top of our mattress. Rush was in his boxers. I was covered head to toe, my socks tucked underneath my leggings to ward off any bugs that might have squeezed their way through the eighty-year-old windows. My mother had called it a "God thing," moving from the city of Oakland to the street with the same name. Her intuition was rarely wrong.

I was lying flat on my back when the anxiety started. It always starts with what I imagine as a premenopausal hot flash, a symptom of quarter-life panic that begins with the sneaking realization that I am on a path. And I don't want to be on a path. I want to zigzag. A warm buzzing in my brain pulses down the base of my head, down the length of my arms, down into the hollow of my belly. Gas fills my ribs like a helium balloon with nowhere to go. It is trapped. I am trapped, unable to breath with this thing pressing out on all sides of me.

"I can't do this," I burst into the silence. "I want to go home."

Rush turned on his side to face me, his eyes as big as the bugs pressed against the screen. "Babe, this is home."

At twenty-six, I believed it was a "God thing" that we were here, fortunate to have this place, fortunate to have each other, but I'd never been persuaded much by gratitude. Gratitude could not keep me in this place any more than gratitude could keep me in my marriage.

≡ ≡ ≡

It's not that I didn't like my marriage. I thought it was a good one. Someone once asked when we'd been married less than a year, "What's the biggest surprise?" and I answered, "How much we laugh." It was a regular routine in our house to use a scratchy kid voice for the pup we adopted and named Amelia Bedelia. Mostly, she said all the things we were thinking but felt too harsh to say, like, "Mom, your toenails are rivaling talons," or "You didn't invite that boozer over again, did you, Dad?" She's even been known to chime in with something crass from under the bed during "sexy time," which, we realized, was profoundly unsexy but made us laugh so hard we gave ourselves double chins. There was depth beneath the laughter, too. If tempers got hot between the two of us, we devised a phrase to defuse the tension. The first person to gain his or her composure would look at the other and say, "I love you, I love you, I love you, I want to be kind." I believed him when he said it. I believed Amelia, too, when she let out a moan from across the room and said, "You two are a couple of saps."

Rush found a new job when we moved to North Carolina, but it came at some loss. He could no longer hop on his fixed-gear bike and sail down Telegraph Avenue like he had in Berkeley, where he worked as a youth pastor for a church we both attended. Now, he took our one and only car and shuttled twenty-five minutes away to a church in a planned development. The staff was smaller and the responsibilities greater. Sunday was no longer just a nighttime commitment to youth group but a fourteen-hour workday. This arrangement left me at the mercy of my bike (and willpower) if I were to get up and out the door in time for a Sunday service of my own. It would be the first time we made our homes at separate churches since marrying.

I could have gone to church with Rush. I could have made it work if I woke up with him on Sunday mornings and covered up in my bathrobe and sat upright in the passenger seat until we arrived at 7:30 a.m. in the empty parking lot. If I had properly dressed myself, I could stay for the early service. I did this once or twice, napping on the couch in his office until 8:30 a.m. Stumbling into the sanctuary with pillow marks on my face wasn't the most graceful of entrances, but it wasn't unworkable. Or I could drop him off and return home to fall asleep again, and make another trip in the evening to attend the 7:00 p.m. service. I'd wait around after it was over for him to shake hands and say his goodbyes. On a good night, we'd be home by 9:00 p.m.

Oh, I tried borrowing friends' cars on occasion, rotating who I asked each week as to not burden anyone, but I soon tired of sending the sheepish text, "You staying in tonight? Mind if I pop on over?" There were Sundays when I didn't even have the energy to make conversation with friends before and after the drop-off. It seemed rude to ask them to leave the keys under the tire.

It wasn't even the time it took each day for two round trips or the amount of fuel we used that kept me away. Those were convenient excuses when I was asked in polite company about why I didn't attend. And it was always, to be sure, a question of why *I* had decided against it, as if Rush was bound to work at a place where we couldn't both worship, and there were no other options except my becoming a good-willed wife. If pressed by close friends, I might share the fact that I wasn't sure what to make of Rush's boss who assured me at a staff barbecue that he supported "women pastors" but seemed uncomfortable with my insistence that feminism at its best wasn't just about supporting women in power but relinquishing the power of privilege. When I pointed out that his position as the male senior pastor over a few female associates wasn't all that uncommon, his eyes shifted toward the blazing bonfire in front of us.

The idea to worship at separate churches seemed logical enough and only mildly subversive at the beginning. I started graduate school a month after we moved into the new house and planned to immerse myself in the local "church scene," as if it were a rollicking pub crawl of professors and pastors sliding me shots of spirituality across the bar. They might ask me to come over for a picnic after church, and I'd decline when they wanted cheap childcare, but we would develop the kind of lifelong friendships that bridged the gap between the classroom and the congregation. Every now and then, I might even invite them over for dinner at our place, and they would marvel when Rush opened our sunny-colored door, "Why, Erin, we didn't even know you had a husband!"

The only problem with this scenario was I wasn't all that motivated to go to the "pub" alone most Sundays. It didn't help that I held the peculiar belief, common among divinity students, that I didn't really need to go to church one day a week when I was studying its founders the other six. Getting started on that outline for St. Gregory of Nyssa's theological anthropology usually did more to quell my anxiety than sitting through a twenty-minute sermon on how I was depraved or

God was love or both. Plus, someone was grading me for the former
and any sort of divine judgment for missing a Sunday or two felt a
long way off.

≡ 4 ≡

A semester of graduate school passed before I went looking for a
church to call my own. Some religion scholars call this activity "church
shopping," but I prefer the term "church dating." Shopping for me is
enjoyable, even satisfying, as I make a list and cross though each item
with the easy stroke of a pen. Sometimes a trip to Whole Foods for
essential oils or Li Ming's for shiitake mushrooms is in order, but
generally I know where to get my needs met and don't have to spend
much time interacting with others to do it. Showing up to my fourth
church in five weeks (admittedly I took a week off for "home church")
was like a round of bad first dates.

For one, I couldn't get the choreography down. It was awkward
when I laughed after saying "trespasses" in a chorus of "debts" during
the Lord's Prayer at a local Presbyterian congregation. It was trou-
bling when I had one eye squinted during communion to survey
whether to dip the wafer or sip the wine at the Emergent church
nearby. And it was defeating when I couldn't even figure out which
door led to the pews and which opened behind the pulpit for all to
see at the Episcopal parish. Having grown up Catholic, I'd been
taught to pick the parish closest to you, but in a town like Durham
this included a surprising array of options if I wasn't limiting myself
to a particular denomination. There was the Friends Meeting that
met in a little brick house near campus and the Southern Baptist
church with a satellite location only a block away, among others. But
perhaps what was most disappointing of all about this whole
courtship was that there was no obvious sign that any of these communities was necessarily *better* than the others. How was I supposed

to know when I found the one? And how long would it be before I got antsy to leave and start someplace new?

Maybe monogamy was my weakness.

⊟ ⊟ ⊟

I never made a checklist, not for finding a church or for finding a partner. I imagine they would have read similarly: must love Jesus—and by extension women—must be smart enough to be my "spiritual leader" and strong enough to know I'll be theirs too, must have a good sense of humor without being too hokey. Children's ministry optional.

It was my mother, a woman my brother nicknamed Perky Patty, or "Perk" for short, who played matchmaker for Rush and me when I was in college. It started with a simple phrase: "When you see him, you'll know." She was sure she heard it from God. And she was sure that God told her it was for me.

"When I see who?" I pressed.

"I don't know."

"I'll know what?" I prodded.

"I don't know."

"Well shoot, Perk, how is this revelation any good to me?"

She chuckled and said with a motherly lack of sympathy, "Honey bun, I just don't know."

I was eighteen when I saw him, striding across the cafeteria floor with a bowl of cereal topped with a yogurt tail. He wasn't my type, small and sturdy, instead of the smoker-skinny men with pants falling off their hips I dated in high school. His skin was bronzed, muddied in appearance, the kind of muddiness that would endear you to a child covered in dirt. Brown waves hit just above his shoulders, kept off his forehead by a bandana. His face was round. His teeth were crooked. His cheeks were dimpled. I had never seen him before, never talked to him, never heard his name. But I *knew*. What I knew though, I just didn't know. It felt like someone had wrapped their hands around my chest and squeezed. It was the kind of squeeze that made you feel safe and the kind that with a slight increase in pressure would surely suffocate.

"I see Jesus in you."

That was my pickup line. I approached him at the altar where he was wrapping up the mic stand from the weekly ecumenical worship service on campus. It was odd. I never so much as mentioned Jesus to a romantic prospect in high school for fear of the good Lord's holiness being one giant turn-off, but now I was using his name as if it was a come-on akin to, "I see Jude Law in you." To be fair, Rush looked like the man behind the "Won by One" poster in my mother's bedroom. He even had a wooly beard that curled just above the collarbone.

"I'd love to grab coffee sometime, if you're free," I offered as his friends threw us sideways glances from the chapel pews. "I'm a freshman and could use a friend who knows the ropes." He didn't know then how lonely I was—that I had started seeing a white-haired therapist my first semester of college to say that it didn't feel right here, people weren't like me here, people were too happy in the South to be trusted.

"Give it time," Dr. Patterson had said. "People can get to eighteen happy, maybe even twenty-one, but everyone has something that breaks them by the time they're thirty."

When Rush and I met for coffee a few days later, I learned that he was a local, so local in fact that he was conceived in the chapel on Main Street where his parents served as caretakers. As if that wasn't enough, he grew up in the town funeral home, which still elicited knocks from grieving strangers. He lived so close to campus that he actually walked to orientation with a bag full of belongings on his back.

It would be another month after that first conversation over coffee before we were officially dating, and once we were a sure thing, I became a sure mess. "Keep me from judging him, from evaluating him, from testing him," I pleaded with God in my tea-stained journal. I asked Rush to call me less on my dorm phone, to brush his teeth before we kissed and to be patient with me as I got used to the fit of my first love. One night we went to one of those make-your-own-pottery places in a nearby town, and I asked, "Which one of us do you think is dating up?" He didn't give an answer, and I didn't know which answer I would have preferred, only that I was the lesser for asking.

My older brother, Charlie, later wondered, "How did you know to stick around if you were so unsure?"

"Oh, I tried to break up with him every other week the first year we dated." I went down the list of complaints aloud, "Too clingy, too cheesy, too short, too passive, funny in all the wrong ways."

"Geez, Erin. Then why did you stay with him?"

"Why did he stay with me?" I joked. I had asked Rush the same thing.

"No, seriously, how did you know?" Charlie asked.

"Because." It was what I told everyone who wanted to know how I knew that he was the one. Not necessarily the only one. But the one I would choose.

"Because running away from him felt like running away from God."

Every other breakup I experienced had been just the opposite: a relief to my anxiety, a rediscovery of self, a returning to God and girl-friends. But when I broke up with Rush, I got the sense I was avoiding someone rather than returning to someone. His love was like alcohol on an open sore. I could either keep picking at familiar scabs or open my body to the sting of healing.

I thought he would make me well.

I thought going to church would do the same.

☲ ☲ ☲

I spent the whole of my two-year program in graduate school speed dating and matchmaking with local churches. None of it worked. While I was mastering theology, I was failing community.

Even for those faithful folks who liked church, it was a rough road to regular attendance. I thought of new friends Juli and Corey, who were having trouble finding a church because none compared to the nondenominational community they left behind. Or Enuma, who travelled so often for work it could be months between visits to the liturgical church that gave her rhythm back home. Then there were Dave and Jenna, who tried their shot with the Quakers and the Universalists and the hippy herbalists but were having a hard time finding a place where they both wanted to plant their naturopathic, home-brewing roots.

There were plenty of good reasons for not showing up at church and, when I did, believing that there wasn't much organized religion had to offer on a Sunday morning that I couldn't get dancing to Florence and the Machine in my living room and giving God a few holy chest thumps.

Some faith communities were better fits than others—that fast-talking preacher who spat on the first row of congregants comes to mind as a particularly bad one, although I did cry the whole way through the altar call. For the most part I believed in the power of "good enough." I believed the research that said too many choices would make me unhappy. I believed in committing to an imperfect partnership and putting in the excruciating work required of it.

W. H. Murray said: "The moment one definitely commits oneself, then Providence moves too."[7]

I just hoped Providence decided to move somewhere within biking distance.

= **5** =

Our church had a going-away party for Rush when we left California for the Carolinas. The students in his ministry got up one by one and said cheeky things like, "What I'll miss most about you is your beard."

The party was probably for me too, but most of my goodbyes had taken place individually, if at all. We had only lived there for two years before I felt the next step in my vocation to be almost three thousand miles away. A parent quipped to Rush as we left the gathering, "I hope you'll finally be able to put down some roots there."

I kept my mouth shut until we were alone in the parking deck beneath the church. "Oh, really? He hopes we'll put down roots someday? And what's so special about roots? Jesus didn't exactly put down roots, you know. Remember that verse about foxholes and nests and not having a pillow?" Catholics aren't known for our memorization of Scripture. "Or what about Paul going to this place and that place? Whatever happened to going where the Spirit moves? If you ask me, I think there are too many adults hung up on roots and not enough of them willing to make like a tree and leave."

As a kid I moved frequently, quitting schools and friendships on demand while my parents quit each other. I quit most boys after a date or two. I quit my first job out of college after three weeks. My first job in high school fared worse, clocking in at only three *hours*. I spent the morning stocking deodorant before the store's air conditioning gave me a runny nose, and I called my mom on my lunch break, heaving, "I'm . . . just . . . so . . . cold." In response to my frequent departures, people often spouted the same lines: "You're so young and idealistic," "Stop being picky," or "Learn to tough it out." It didn't take long before my peers were raising their eyebrows, too, asking what my decisions would look like on a resume. Quitting was a sign of immaturity rather than one of personality—even if it was a personality defect in their view.

I tried to quit Rush, too. We weren't engaged long before I started panicking, worried that marriage would clip my wings before they were fully grown. I wanted to move to California, try my hand as a writer, maybe even become a pastor or a soap-opera star. I joined the performance of the *Vagina Monologues* my senior year and developed a crush on the director, a veiny man in his forties with gelled hair and leather jackets who kissed me on my forehead and asked me to tell him about Jesus. After one session of premarital counseling, Reverend Lowell looked at me and said, "Should you really be wearing that ring?"

A friend's parent consoled me, "It's better to marry young before you're set in your ways. You become adults together."

I wondered when I would find time to become myself.

⊟ ⊟ ⊟

Not long after we married, I dragged Rush to a retreat with me on the four natural elements of success.[8] It was one of those personality assessments that doled out labels for the very thing that can never be captured in a number or combination of letters. Of course, it is nice to be told this is how you are and this is how you are not. I never know though if I'm a trustworthy judge of character, my own especially. (An old mentor emails me, "How's your relationship with Jesus?" and I respond, "I don't know. Ask him.")

There was something different about the four elements, though, that stuck with me even as the letters of the personality law fell away. Each element—earth, wind, fire and water—had multiple facets to it. Fire wasn't just angry and powerful; it could be warm and crackling. Earth wasn't just steady and supportive; it could be stubborn and cautious. Rush's kindred element of water symbolized his "go with the flow" likeability but also his tendency to be overly sensitive to the gales of change.

One of the women helping to lead the retreat was a petite southerner with cockatoo-blond hair and punch-pink lipstick. She shared how she and her husband used to own a print shop together. She liked the work and enjoyed talking to the customers, but each day the mailman came in the office, dropped off the mail and walked back out the door, and each day she would think to herself, "What I wouldn't give to be the mailman."

I knew exactly what she meant.

I wanted to be like the wind, too, always on the move, never fully grasped. Moody, the wind doesn't appear to have a reason behind which leaf it rips through in summer or why it breaks harshly against your face at night. It is violent, though you'd never believe it. It is present, though you'd strain to see it. One does not say that the wind has quit, only that it has died in this place and is blowing through to the next. It howls with longing.

Some say that longing created the world. Sixteenth-century German theologian Jacob Boehme interpreted the creation story as beginning with a "concentration of desire." It was desire that was the first something out of nothing, and it was the "insatiability of the desiring" that put in motion the creation of the world.[9] Perhaps it was God's own longing that catalyzed the wind over the waters (Genesis 1:2) and called the ground into being (Genesis 1:9).

I learned a funny thing when we moved to North Carolina and bought our house on Oakland Avenue. Maybe you know it too. When you buy a house you technically own the land, but you also own some of the vertical space above and below your land. It's a centuries old idea that comes from the Latin phrase *Cuius est solum, eius est usque ad coelum et ad inferos,* which means "whoever owns the soil, it is theirs up to heaven and down to hell." Not until the Wright brothers began crisscrossing the boundaries of American airspace at the beginning of the twentieth century did the federal government amend ownership of the air above one's house to "within the range of actual occupation." By 1946, the Supreme Court had deemed such airspace a virtual "highway" above our heads, despite complaints from one Mr. Crausby of Greensboro, North Carolina, that World War II fighter jets had flown so low over his house that his chickens were sent into a suicidal panic.[10] Surely, this is a silly notion to anyone who thinks about it too long. Owning air. Air belongs to everyone—and to no one.

Still, I wondered, is it even possible for the wind to have roots? I worried I was incapable. I worried more that I wasn't.

I attend Outpost Community Church once or twice before deciding that it's a serious prospect. It is the kind of place that makes you take a second look after you compare it to other suitors. You'll have to forgive its annoying quirks. But perhaps you hadn't had the complete picture when you first met.

I try to give it a real go this time in the hopes that I might catch a glimpse of the Spirit, the lingering presence of God that has me scheming for ways to catch it in its natural habitat. This church seems to be one of those places.

Outpost has two primary things going for it: (1) I can bike to it and, from what I surmise, most people who go here can do the same, and (2) said people seem to *care*. It isn't that they care about the right stuff (my stuff) but that they care about caring for each other. These criteria seem sufficient.

When I walk into the sanctuary with its honey-colored walls and stately pillars, I see Bess sitting in the pastors' pew, her petite body wrapped in marled yarn. A southern woman, raised in Waco and married to an Oklahoman, Bess entered the ordination process while working as an intern at Outpost. I think her courageous. She lives in one of the poorest neighborhoods in Durham. She watches the two little boys down the block when their mother runs to the store. She attends the art opening of the woman who shares her duplex. She knows the names of the homeless men who stand outside the church and expects them to learn her name, too, if they are going to be real friends. She even tells them so, pressing her small, heart-shaped face close to theirs.

Bess and I became close in graduate school. We met in the opening chapel service and quickly discovered that we both liked to bike. The following day we made plans to ride to school together like some middle-school gang. All that was missing were the playing cards fixed to our spokes by clothespins. There were other things we held in common, too. In addition to staving off addictions to sugar-free gum and Diet Coke, we loved talking theological trash. We'd be walking around the perimeter of campus, and I'd say something about how taking communion helps me remember who I am, and she'd say something like, "You could get into a lot of trouble with that kind of sentimental hogwash." Maybe that is another reason I am here, too; a young woman like me isn't just in the pulpit but walking around giving name tags and shaking hands and acting like there is nowhere else she belongs more.

I told Bess I would commit to coming to Outpost for the summer. An end date for commitment is like a lifeboat to one terrified of time's expanse. Twelve weeks of going to the same church with plenty of Sundays off for summer travel? I can swing this. Plus, I hope it will appease Bess, who has always been wary of my critiques of the church lobbed from the safe distance of a blog post. Better to actually build something up from the inside than tear it down from the outside.

My first Sunday back at Outpost, I notice three things:

One, it is a singing congregation. The worship leader, an older man with box-framed glasses, shouts out instructions to the congregation over the top of his piano. It's ridiculous—shouldn't someone give him a mic?—but the voices around me are so strong one has to strain to hear herself.

Two, it is a dancing congregation. This mainline, Protestant congregation is full of clappers, the type of folk who are always an eighth of a beat too late but look so happy doing it that one forgives them their clumsiness. They clap and sway and even put their hands up like Perk does when she's really feeling the Spirit.

Three, it is a peace-passing congregation. When it comes time to shake hands with a room full of strangers, people actually get out of their seats—and even their rows!—to shuffle around the sanctuary giving blessing upon blessing. They even make an effort to learn my name and stick their hands out without being all smarmy.

The people are so earnest here that I try not to focus too much on the fact that we are mostly a bunch of white folks in a city where two-thirds of the population is black or Latino. I try not to be too critical that they don't bother to make the language gender neutral in the prayer of confession, let alone in the sermon or songs. I try not to think about it too hard when we kneel and say that we are depraved, that "there is no health in us," even now, even with all this grace. The people are so earnest, in fact, that I nearly forget to care about any theological differences we have.

We celebrate Pentecost, the occasion for the Holy Spirit descending on the apostles in the first century A.D. and causing a flurry of miracles and misunderstanding. The day marks the fulfillment of not only Christ's promise to dwell with his followers and equip them for service in the world but also the vision of the prophet Joel who testified on behalf of God to all of Israel: "I will pour out my spirit on all flesh; your sons and your daughters shall prophesy" (Joel 2:28). The message of Pentecost was one for Jews and its converts alike, both those who belonged to the original covenant and those wondering if they could be adopted in.

And it all began with a sound from heaven and a hungry wind.

= 7 =

I take to calling the next year of my life my "first third year." It's the first time I've hit the two-year mark in a city with no plan to move. The list of possible places is becoming shorter; Seattle remains, and Milwaukee is in the running, but Boulder seems too isolated now to stomach. Columbus has the best ice cream I've ever tasted, but I bought the recipe book from my favorite shop and can now make a mean goat cheese and cherry concoction of my own.

The Monday after I return to Outpost, I am driving to the outdoor mall when I hear an interview on the radio with one of those young professionals who has been on the go ever since leaving home. He moves around, almost every year, sometimes multiple times a year, for really important stuff, the stuff that you'd be proud to put in your alumni journal. He says something like, "The minute I stop moving, life stops being an adventure." I might have given him a high five a few years ago. Now I wonder, *What if the adventure is staying put?*

It occurs to me it's the adventure I haven't tried.

Lesson Two

THE ART OF
READING CHARITABLY

The mind that is not baffled is not employed.
The impeded stream is the one that sings.

WENDELL BERRY

Sweat is the oil of summer in Durham. It pumps the legs that pump the bicycles and pump the bugs full of blood. Outside the air is as thick as a hand-cut piece of bacon, and just as greasy. The grass smells feral; so, too, does Amelia Bedelia when she comes in fresh from a face plant in Oval Park. Dead cicadas glisten on the sidewalk. Ice cream sticks to fingers, and shorts stick to thighs. Stillness brings death to the garden planted in spring with possibilities.

This seems hardly the time to start fresh.

Cynics claim to make our home in reality, but it is often the reality of the past that we project onto the future with certainty. According to Jim Wallis, cynicism is a "spiritually dangerous thing" because it prevents us from making meaningful commitments.[1] How can we commit when we are convinced that there can be no change in what will be but only a rehearsal of what has been? It is why we hedge our bets, play our cards and try not to let our hopes fly when considering with whom we'll share a life. It is how we find our grown selves looking around a room one day and admitting, "I don't even know how to belong."

I don't even know where to begin.

And so I begin at Outpost Community Church like I always begin. I begin by looking for a fight. It is what I did dating my husband. It is what I did growing up in the church. After years of resisting commitment, can I even let myself belong to others?

Summer has just started perspiring when I sign up for a six-week marriage class. This seems like taking a vegan boyfriend to a southern pig pickin' just to get a rise. Here my inner cynic will be itching to come out. Here she'll feast on a buffet of wounds. Here I hope she'll find a bite of charity.

≡ ≡ ≡

The notice for the class runs in the June bulletin at Outpost. A course on Tim and Kathy Keller's book, *The Meaning of Marriage*, promises to "help us develop a biblical and realistic vision of marriage, make good choices and face the complexities of commitment with the wisdom of God." Outpost's senior pastor, Martin, and his wife, Cynthia, will lead the study, along with a cast of other dutiful duos.

The first Meaning of Marriage class falls on one of those rare Sundays Rush has off from work, and we decide to travel to the Blue Ridge Mountains to visit our friends Jason and Jaylynn. We like these two—so much, in fact, that they're on an actual pen-and-paper list of our favorite couples. Jason, a writer and wordsmith, might poke at Jaylynn's Texan slang, and Jaylynn might roll her eyes at Jason's over-thought theology, but under the smirks and sighs there's a current of respect. A little slice of sanity left when they moved across the state last year with their three boys.

As Rush and I drive through the Yadkin Valley and up into the foothills, our anticipation rises with the altitude. We're greeted at their split-level parsonage with hugs from our friends and curious stares from the boys; only the oldest seems to remember playing in our office while the adults nursed mimosas. "We splurged on a babysitter," Jaylynn says with a grin.

Dinner is in an old jail converted into a hipster haven where home fries are served instead of French fries and no-name soda replaces catchall Coke. Rush orders too much, and I compensate by ordering too little. Jason and Jaylynn take turns waving at the stream of local folks who come in and out of the packed dining room. It's a hazard of the job—Jason a senior pastor of a large university church and Jaylynn a solo pastor at two smaller ones.

"What's it like?" I ask them, sliding a potato skin off Rush's plate and into my mouth. "Not worshiping in the same place?"

Jaylynn answers first. "We've done it before. Pastored multiple churches. We know how to do it. But it's different with our three boys getting older. They take turns going to Jason's church with a sitter or tagging along with me to two services."

"And you? What do your Sunday mornings look like?"

She lets out a throaty laugh. "I love my churches, I do. I'm learning so much about this mountain culture and its people by knowing these small churches and their generations of families. And my boys get to experience the small church in a way they may never have the chance to again."

Rush puts his hand on my leg and gives it a squeeze. "I love the church where I work, but I get why Erin's not there."

"You wouldn't choose to go to Rush's church if you could?" Jason prods me from across the table, taking a sip of his brown-bottled beer.

"Well, no. Not now at least," I admit. Turning to Rush, I explain, as if talking about his best friend or, worse, our sex life, "There's just no spark for me there."

I look for his cue to continue, and he nods. "I'm worried, though, that going to separate churches isn't sustainable for us in the long run. Not sure what that means yet."

Jaylynn replies without a lick of pity, "We're praying for longevity, too."

Later that night, my feet tucked under the quilt in our basement bedroom, I poke Rush with my big toe. "Erin, what did I tell you? Warn me next time you're going to touch me with those ice cubes."

"Sorry, I forgot," I say and burrow my whole foot beneath his calf for warmth. "Can I ask you a question?" He hates when I ask this question. It makes him nervous.

"What do you think about heading home a little early so we can go to my new church on Sunday?" My foot squirms under the weight of his body. "Could be nice."

He puts down his *Sports Illustrated* and looks at me with a blank stare. It's a ridiculous request, I'm sure, asking a pastor if he'd like to worship at a different church on his day off, like asking a landscaper if it'd be fun to putter around in someone else's yard on the weekend. Still, he wouldn't say no. He so rarely says no. "Okay," he agrees after a beat. "If it's important to you, babe, I'll go."

"Oh, good." I slide my foot out from under him and turn toward the wall before it can be settled differently. The corner of my mouth pressed firmly into my lace-trimmed pillow, I mumble a few final words, "And while we're there, we'll go to a marriage class too."

≈ 9 ≈

I make sure to grab my wedding ring off the ledge near the toilet before Rush and I head out the door. The Meaning of Marriage class takes place during the Sunday school hour between the two morning services; it'll be Rush's first glimpse into my new community. When we arrive in the fellowship hall before worship, I am chattier than usual. Turning to the couple behind me, who look to be in their forties or fifties, I ask how long they have been together. Almost twenty years, they say, and I wonder aloud how they are going to celebrate. They turn to one another and shrug.

There's a group of about fifty folks gathered in the alpine-shaped room, from young people in plastic-framed glasses to older folks who sit with speckled hands crossed. We spot Bess's husband, Henry, a skinny young man with khaki pants rolled to the ankles and thick, slick, Superman hair. She and I often commiserate about the ease with which our mates move in the church. We drive ourselves mad second-guessing our every word, earning trust like stockbrokers reading the market. For men like Henry and Rush, trust may as well have been dropped off at their doorsteps in canvas sacks with money signs. Could we complain if we enjoyed the spoils?

Henry comes over to the row where the two of us are sitting and gives Rush a pat on the back. "Good to see you, man. You off today?"

"I am, my friend, I am," Rush says.

"What are you doing here?" I ask. "Is Bess coming?"

"Nah. Just me. I thought it'd be interesting." His eyes wander toward the other side of the room where a small group of people huddles around the coffeepot.

"Did you buy the book? We bought the book." I run my hand along the hardback spine and wonder if my graduation gift card was well spent. Maybe I should have bought a puppy calendar instead.

He shakes his head and laughs. "There's no way I'm reading that book."

When class begins, I'm already coaching myself to keep calm. A blazer-clad man with unsettling diction welcomes the now-packed room of laity, and I wonder why he insists on being such a showoff. Next come a few words from Cynthia, who assures us, "*We* are not the experts," and while I'm prone to letting my petty thoughts run free, she steadies my anxiety with her low voice, no-nonsense bob and dry sense of humor that comes out not the least bit slanted. Even though I don't want to heave onto her the same expectation of likeability I have wrestled as a pastor's wife, who she is matters. Who she is reveals what matters to Martin.

Finally, Martin approaches the podium, his gray suit coat flapping gently behind him. He's the picture of the pastor-type. An inoffensive shape. An authoritative head of hair. A permanent half smile. He has the well-worn confidence that comes with age and the respect of a congregation he's led for decades. He even has what I'll come to recognize as a well-worn rhetoric: Tell them how the world is. Tell them how Jesus is. Now tell them how to be like Jesus in the world.

冃 冃 冃

"The world offers a sorry picture of commitment," Martin begins. "The divorce rate is twice what it was fifty years ago, children are being born out of wedlock in staggering numbers, and only half the population is married as compared to almost three-fourths in 1960."[2] Nowadays, he explains, marriage is typically construed as a boring, unhappy and draining relationship of only some social utility.

Although Martin laments that his generation of the sixties wild child "was the starting point for when everything went south," younger generations like mine shoulder much of the blame for treating relationships like a rotating playlist of preference. Commitments are no longer driven by our desire to fulfill a duty but to fulfill ourselves. In part, this makes us, according to a *Time* magazine cover story, the "most threatening and exciting generation since the baby boomers brought about social revolution, not because [we're] trying to take over the Establishment but because [we're] growing up without one."[3]

I was in high school when the twin towers of the World Trade Center returned to dust on the television screen. By college we were at war, and have been ever since from how it seems, political rhetoric notwithstanding. But before all that there was a divorce to deal with, and I remember feeling like I knew more than I should for an eight-year-old. Dad moved back to Detroit, and Mom put us on a plane out of Chicago every other weekend to see him. Unaccompanied minors. Wings were our reward.

There was 533 Ravine Drive and 911 Ellis Street and one house I can't remember in between before Perk got a message from God to pack up and move out to be near Dad. No more missed volleyball tournaments on the weekend or missed layovers in Cleveland.

"What do you think, Charlie?" she asked.

"Fine by me."

"And, Erin?"

"The Taras haven't been all that nice to me lately."

There was no job waiting for her when we arrived in Ann Arbor, just a two-bedroom apartment—one room for the boxes, one room for the three of us. The cat ran away in Battle Creek, but oh, it was a blessed year making a life with two real parents. At the end of the year, Dad announced he was moving to California with his wife. You never forgave me that, he'll say years later, but he'll be wrong.

The winters were an ugly shade of mud in Michigan, and so were the frat parties my best friend, Lia, and I snuck into on the weekends. When it came time to choose a college, I flipped through the *Princeton Review*'s rankings and circled the schools in the "northern south"—North Carolina, Virginia, D.C. The red brick and white columns promised an untarnished home, a home that smelled like laundry and lawn. When I graduated four years later, my college career counselor handed me a sheet of paper that read, "Possible Jobs for Anthropology Majors," but it didn't help a lick. By twenty-two, we were supposed to know how to get the life we wanted. Or the life we should want. We could hardly tell the difference.

Whether we went to college or not, we expected there would be jobs enough for everyone. I started a full-time position as a book publicist in San Francisco three weeks before Lehman Brothers filed for bankruptcy and the economy began to unravel. I went to New York City for training in September. Each morning I walked to and from the train station from my hotel in Times Square, and each morning I saw men and women carrying cardboard boxes out of revolving doors.

Experts argue about whether the instability we've experienced—from the collapse of the World Trade Center to the collapse of the economy—makes us psychologically different from the generations before us. According to researcher Jeffrey Jensen Arnett, there is a developmental stage unique to our times called "emerging adulthood," a period "during which young people are no longer adolescents but have not yet attained full adult status."[4] Soft on responsibility. High on narcissism. Delaying, delaying, delaying the pressures of adulthood. Some say we were coddled and cuddled and given one too many trophies for participation.

I say we're scared out of our minds to be disappointed.

While my middle- to upper-class peers have been criticized as affiliation-averse, commitment-phobic wanderers who would rather find themselves on a trip to India than in a church in Iowa, the picture of belonging across economic lines is more complex. In an op-ed in the *New York Times* called "Young and Isolated," Jennifer Silva describes the reality of working-class blacks and whites she studied in Lowell, Massachusetts, and Richmond, Virginia:

> These are people bouncing from one temporary job to the next; dropping out of college because they can't figure out financial aid forms or fulfill their major requirements; relying on credit cards for medical emergencies; and avoiding romantic commitments because they can take care of only themselves. Increasingly disconnected from institutions of work, family and community, they grow up by learning that counting on others will only hurt them in the end. Adulthood is not simply being delayed but dramatically re-imagined along lines of trust, dignity, and connection and obligation to others.[5]

Apathetic? Hardly. Heartbroken is more like it. We were taught we could be anything we wanted to be—by advertisers, yes, but by well-meaning teachers and parents, too. Nevermind that the deck was stacked against us if our bodies were brown, poor, queer or disabled. Success was in our grasp if only we tried harder, always just a little harder. Everything seemed possible, until it wasn't.

Perhaps the fact that only 20 percent of young people ages 18 to 29 are married[6] is not a sign of moral laxity but fear. We became adults during a widespread epidemic of mistrust in both each other and the institutions that were meant to support us. While belief in God remains steady in the United States, confidence in the religious institutions that provide scaffolding for such belief is near its lowest point in decades.[7] Nowadays, Americans have more confidence in the military than they do in the church.

We are a generation trapped between the twin terrors of freedom and fear. Trapped, Tim Keller writes in his book, "between both unrealistic longings for and terrible fears about marriage."[8] He may as well be talking about the church. For many of us, church has become—like marriage—another institution in which we have high hopes but little confidence.

We want too much and not nearly enough from it.

There has to be another way.

≡ ≡ ≡

I lean forward and grip the lip of my chair as Martin turns our attention to the *sine qua non* of marriage passages. He jokes that despite having performed over 250 marriage ceremonies, he's only been asked to preach on the fifth chapter of Ephesians twice. In it, wives are encouraged to submit to their husbands as to the Lord, and husbands are charged to love their wives as Christ loves the church. But we miss a crucial clue to life together if we don't read on past the point of comfort to the end of the passage. The writer says he's not really talking about marriage. Marriage is a metaphor for something else. In Ephesians 5:31-32 (NIV), he writes, "'A man will leave his father and mother and be united to his wife, and the two will become one flesh.' This is a profound mystery—but I am talking about Christ and the church."

One flesh. Not just me and Rush but Christ and the church. What does it mean for us to be one flesh with a body that by all biblical accounts is resurrected? The Greek word used for unity in Ephesians is transliterated into *henotes* (Ephesians 4:3, 13); its root signifies "oneness," oneness between the persons of the Trinity but also our oneness with God and each other.[9] The author describes this oneness as the "bond of peace" (Ephesians 4:3), but it's not a bond made smooth by smiles and swallowed words. It's a bond that requires the charge of opposites to work in harmony, like electrons dancing around protons and pulling each other close. To be one flesh with a living body means that, for a marriage to mend or a church to unify, the dead skin of cynicism will have to fall off.

Martin slows his words for emphasis, "This is not a contractual agreement that says I'll stay with you as long as my needs are met. It's a covenant relationship where together you are seeking something more than your own happiness." *Covenant* is the biblical word for a long-term commitment in which a gift is promised by God and we respond with a promise of our own.[10] We make a choice to limit our options to this God, this partner, this church, trusting that with promise paradoxically comes a new kind of freedom. Freedom *from* the tyranny of choice. Freedom *for* the intimacy of choosing one.

I want to be free of my flaky fear, I do. I have tried to trust God for as much; this is the God of the universe after all, a God who according to our Scriptures has a cynic-sloughing kind of love. But humans are a different story. Humans write marriage books in which the mystery and metaphor of husband and wife are an ironclad prescription for *all* relationships; women are rarely typed as the Christ and men never pursued as his bride. Humans teach marriage classes in which they lament the selfishness of birth control with nary an affirmation, ahem, of childfree couples and their life of service. Humans say things to my khaki-shorted, flip-flopped husband after class like, "They let you get away with wearing *that* to work in Chapel Hill?"

Humans have what my friend Pilar calls the "body of Christ odor," and my B.O. detector is on high alert.

I try to stay open, open to it all, to the really good things I hear during class and the really irksome things that make me want to run for the door. I even try to stay open to my inner cynic, offering the poor girl some sympathy when she says on our way out, "They don't really get it," and I say back, "Neither do you, dear."

The whole thing requires a sort of mindfulness practice like the one I learned in yoga class. "Just notice the thought," Curry would say as we folded into ourselves with stiff knees. "Don't judge it. Don't condemn it. Acknowledge it." And with the next exhale we would release it.

Or the next one.

We'd get there. Breath by breath.

Exhaling the thought excrement.

Inhaling the odor of life in the body.

= 10 =

Egyptian priests were the first known perfumers in the world. From them the ancient Jews learned the practices of anointing bodies with unguents and preparing fragrance for worship. Archaeological evidence dating back to the first century reveals a sort of perfume workshop in service of the nearby temple in Jerusalem. Extracting odors from the earth, whether in the form of flowers or honey or wine, and turning them into vapor was thought to mediate the opposing worlds of spirit and matter. Rooted in the ancient art of alchemy, the process transformed raw material into a mysterious substance that was somehow purer, more unified, than the sum of its parts.[11] Ordinary metal was put to the test and spun into gold.

This is how church works, too.

ᗗ ᗗ ᗗ

I can still smell the cloak of incense that followed them down the center aisle. They came two by two, dressed like white petit fours with crisp, scalloped edges. I tucked my legs up on the pew and came to a standing position for a better view. What looked like a mass parade of miniature brides and grooms marched by me. They were second graders about to receive their first holy communion, and I was a jealous five-year-old.

As I watched them process, Dad put his hand on my shoulder. He didn't ask me to get down. Neither did Mom. I could color on my forearms, play MASH on the back of the bulletin or fall asleep with my body sprawled across the pew without reprimand. If I asked for a backrub during Mass, they would give in, making the time between the liturgist and the homily pass quickly. Barring any truly obnoxious behavior, we'd get to stop off at Dunkin Donuts on the way home. The rest of the family eventually tired of the treats, but I insisted on getting dropped off, running in each week to see if the color of sprinkles had changed for the upcoming holiday.

I spotted my brother quickly. The warm light from Our Lady of Humility's stained glass bounced off his wire-framed glasses. I wrangled myself away from Dad's grip and jumped to the ground so I could catch his attention as he passed.

"Charlie!" I whispered with the hoarseness of a child's "inside voice."

He raised one cheek and then the other like a wave to lift his glasses higher on his face. Seeing it was me, he unhooked his arm from the Hispanic girl beside him and waved. I spun around to face my Dad, grabbing his cheek for leverage. "Look, Dad. It's Charlie."

The whole congregation gazed approvingly as the little ones gathered around the altar for the ceremony. "Father, bless these children and make them eager to share in the banquet of Jesus," the laity recited dutifully. I watched the Communion wafer placed on each tiny tongue and the chalice raised to each tiny lip, and for the first time in my life, I watched without fidgeting.

"Mom, why do I have to wait until I'm in the second grade to have Communion?" I asked back at home, feet dangling off a kitchen stool, fingers still sticky from the donut.

"That's a good question, honey bun," she said with a twang in her voice as she pulled a Styrofoam tray of ground beef out of the freezer and banged it against the side of the cabinet.

"It doesn't make sense," I whined. "I understand as much as Charlie does. Jesus died on the cross. And to remember it we eat him and drink him. Like supper."

Perk stopped near the oven and wiped her hands with a dish-towel. "That's right, Miss E. Just like the Last Supper. You think they ate donuts back then?"

"They didn't eat donuts back then, silly. They had bread and wine. Red wine," I said laughing, pulling the skin down beneath my eyes for added emphasis. Dad had given me a taste of the Kool-Aid-looking stuff in my kid cup once. I didn't care much for the flavor, but I expected Jesus juice was a cut above the grocery store variety.

"Well, bunky, if you think you're ready, then I don't see why not. I'll call over to the church on Monday." And with that, she smiled, lifted the mass of meat up once more and gave it a final thwack.

⊟ ⊟ ⊟

Growing up, Perk was the binoculars through which I understood the shape of God. Through this lens, God was a labor and delivery nurse. God smelled like powder. God changed the oil. God liked a clean bathroom. God was a champion Hula-Hooper. God drove a church bus. God handled snakes, mice and hermit crabs. God was sensitive but couldn't be manipulated. God spoke with nasally pluck. And God sung along to The Chiffons on the oldies station.

Sure, we called God "our Father" and understood Jesus to be "his only Son," but I tried picturing this God when I tossed around in bed at night, and all that came to mind was Santa with his twisty white tufts. When nightmares of the witch from Snow White kept me awake, I superimposed Perk's face on the bodiless God, who I petitioned for world peace and a brood of Cabbage Patch Kids. Still, when I'm tangled by the image of a peppered Poseidon in the sky, I picture Perk with her mauve glasses and bleached blond hair.

God seems kinder and funnier this way.

Perk was ninety pounds when she got married. The pictures show her with feathered hair, ginger skin and a round-toothed grin. A nominal Christian when they met, she promised Dad to raise the future kids Catholic. She couldn't have known that she would become "born again" some five years later when we were still banging around in diapers. But despite her charismatic awakening, Perk passed along the Catholic faith to us; she even converted to Catholicism. I don't know what compelled her conversion, only that she wasn't all that stuck on semantics. A Catholic was a kind of Christian, and if the kids were to become Catholic, then she would, too.

⊟ ⊟ ⊟

A few weeks after our kitchen conversation, Perk set up a meeting at Our Lady of Humility with Marlena Porter, a tan and gregarious Midwesterner who was the head of religious education. The two of us sat alone in a classroom, a large laminate table between us. If there were pleasantries, I don't remember. Mostly there were questions.

Who do you receive when you receive the Eucharist?

What is happening when the priest blesses the bread and wine?

How should you prepare to welcome Jesus into your body?

I can't imagine how theologically sophisticated my answers were at age five. But I knew something then. I knew that you didn't have to know much to belong to Christ's body. You just had to want it real bad.

By the end of our conversation, Marlena agreed that I knew what I wanted. Together we returned to the church office where she picked up the phone and called Father Joe. "I've got a five-year-old here who's ready to take her first Holy Communion. How soon can we do this?"

Perk chose Mother's Day. When the morning Masses were over and the mothers home with their long-stemmed roses, I had my own private Communion ceremony at Our Lady of Humility and asked my Jewish friend Sarah Shapiro to celebrate with me. This was as evangelistic as I'd ever get. Come see the magic, bread turned into flesh, wine turned into blood, sinners turned into saints; can you believe it's all real? I had Jesus coursing through my veins.

When we returned home, I did cartwheels down our condominium driveway in my elbow-length gloves. This seemed the dignified thing to do. Marlena Porter allowed me more than my First Communion that day. She allowed me to witness my own strength and the strength of the church to endure me. Sure, sometimes when I'd go to receive Communion in the days after, some deacon who thought I looked too young would pat me on the head and send me into a holy fit. But I learned there were some things worth fighting for. The body of Christ was one of them.

"Opposition," John O'Donohue wrote, "forces our abilities to awaken; it tests the temper and substance of who we are."[12] If it does not break us, we stand a chance of shining.

⟨11⟩

Rush and I are taking turns reading *The Meaning of Marriage* at night despite only having made it to one class so far. I read a chapter. He reads a chapter. I read another chapter, and another. Then I make some comment about it, and he catches up.

"You know my biggest beef with this book?" Rush asks as he rolls over on his side in bed and props his body up next to mine.

I can think of a number of beefs I have with this book. But, no, I can't think to which one my far less critical partner is referring.

"I just don't hear Kathy in this book. Where's a woman's perspective? Where's a woman's voice?" His eyes get wider and bluer, and in all seriousness he almost whimpers, "Where's Kathy?"

There's only one chapter explicitly written by Kathy Keller, and it's on the differences in "divinely assigned gender roles." Throughout the rest of the book women are portrayed as angry ex-girlfriends, hurt and hampered wives, pleading daughters, and regretful mistresses. Human friendship is lifted up with the examples of male-buddy movies like *The Dirty Dozen* or *Lord of the Rings*. There is no *Sex and the City* or *Sisterhood of the Traveling Pants*. An example of why a relationship falls apart is when "a woman 'lets herself go' or a man loses his job." After all, the book reminds us, "Most of us know that there is some truth in the stereotype that men overvalue beauty in a prospective spouse and that women overvalue wealth in a potential mate."[13] I understand Tim is the pastor. I understand Tim is the writer. I understand Tim is the sell. I understand why he gets top billing. What I don't understand is why—if men and women are so fundamentally different—isn't it that much more necessary for their perspectives to be shared equally in literature, sermons and conversations? Too often I hear men in leadership speaking for and about their wives, mothers and daughters instead of hearing from those very women themselves. It is as if the church speaks with one (male) voice, as if gender differences don't matter after all. So which is it?

⊟ ⊟ ⊟

I already know something of Tim Keller. Tim is the kind of pastor-man other pastor-men love. Our premarital counselor, Reverend Lowell, was a big fan; every college couple who came to him curious about how far was too far, when was the "right time" to get married or whose career should come first got pointed toward Tim and his theory on gender differences. "Marriage is a dance," Reverend Lowell would say. "In order to move together, the man leads and the woman follows, but there is no assignment of worth. Both are necessary for the intimacy and order of marriage." I thought to ask him why intimacy couldn't be freestyled, or why we couldn't switch up our moves depending on the song. Still, despite all his efforts to persuade me, Reverend Lowell was quick to admit, "A Christian might have good theology and still remain an insufferable a**."

His gentle conviction helped me articulate my own with civility. It was not without thought, after all, that Rush and I asked a man with whom we fundamentally disagreed on the role of husband and wife to coofficiate our wedding. No talk of being fruitful and multiplying, please. No blessing of future offspring, thank you. No introduction of the couple as man and wife, but Rush and Erin. Speak to us instead, we said, about the ministry of reconciliation.

The idea of divinely assigned gender roles fascinated me in my early years at college, like a toddler who's discovered her reflection in a bent spoon; I could make some sense of myself, even if the image was warped. While I would have argued with you over whether women were gifted to have "authority over men" as I did with Reverend Lowell, I conceded that there were some discernible patterns to being a man and a woman that might not be chalked up to differences in upbringing and socialization alone. Like the personality tests that satisfy our curiosity for why we are the way we are, many of the generalizations about men and women do the same. What start out as broad brushstrokes that help to explain a pattern of *some* men or *some* women can end up painting *all* of us into a corner. Dorothy Sayers, mystery writer and noted friend of C. S. Lewis, addressed her audience in 1938 with these prophetic words: "We are much too inclined these days to divide people into permanent categories, forgetting that a category only exists for its special purpose and must be forgotten as soon as that purpose is served."[14]

As much as I enjoyed the mild winters of the "northern south" when I first arrived at college, the mild manners were harder to get used to. A few of my freshman girlfriends blushed when I dropped a swear word. When it came to the dating rituals on campus, I whined to my mom, "The boys spend so much time praying about making a move that virtually no moves are being made." Once, I walked up to a billowing young man at a frat party and yelled in his ear, "You're really good looking." He took his hands out of his pocket and bent down to face me. "And you must be from the North." It was a relief to find people at college who shared my faith values, but I was perplexed by some of the gendered values that came with it. I didn't know being mad was a character flaw in a woman.

I remember calling Perk when I first met Rush, fretting over whether it was out of line to ask him out. What if I started a precedent for being the initiator? What if—horrors—the singular act of my pick-up line doomed the rest of our imaginary romance to a pattern? Like many college-aged girls in the early 2000s, I had read John Eldredge's wildly popular *Wild at Heart* and worried the news was true: men needed an adventure and I needed rescuing.

"Remember how in high school your friends called you 'the cruise director'?" Perk asked. My brain was wired for planning, organizing and words like *calendaring*. It pained me to see a decision that needed to be made and a group too polite to be decisive. Waffling was about as attractive to me as it sounded. "Initiating is your gift, bunky, and if you go off and start being someone else, what's God supposed to do with that? God needs you to be you, Erin." I wasn't sure God needed anything from me, but I liked the thought.

At nineteen I found my first gray hair, and this seemed fitting. The more I thought about "divinely assigned gender roles" the less they fit the graying reality I experienced as I grew older. Even biological categories of male and female proved problematic as I learned about the reality of intersex individuals, who by virtue of their hormones, chromosomes and anatomy don't fit neatly into our conventional categories.[15] Could we chalk their lives up to aberrations like we did women who sought the thrill of the chase? Of course men needed an adventure, but I, too, loved playing capture the flag in the dark or scheming over how to prank the dry dorm. And sure, women needed to be pursued, but Rush loved it when I told him, "Clear your schedule. I've got something planned." If there were differences the Christian should be pointing out, it was the structural differences that were keeping women out of the pulpit and men from taking paternity leave. Perhaps the writings of Christians like John Eldredge and the Kellers resonate with folks not because they are pinpointing the innate differences between men and women but because they are accurately describing human nature—with its universal desire to know and be known—even if they are parsing it between two halves of a whole.

It's hard to abide these kinds of half-truths coming from a Christian book or pulpit. I suppose we all are prone to speaking in half-truths. Maybe to call it "half-truth" is even generous. Maybe we deal more in halfpence-truths. But the more I grew out of the stereotypes that disguised themselves as stable identity markers of Christian men and women, the more my connection to the church became, well, unstable.

ⴹ ⴹ ⴹ

It begs the question: What am I doing now at Outpost where the public leadership is still largely male? It's the best reason I can give friends who know my story and wonder why I'm here. And it is a hard one to argue.

"Each week I walk into the sanctuary, I feel the Holy Spirit."

I can't explain it any other way, really. At Outpost I experience the presence of God viscerally, if not theologically. Goosebumps during worship. Tears during the children's liturgy. And sure enough when I make it to the next marriage class, my breath quickens and my chest tightens, and I am reminded of my kindling conviction.

= 12 =

I don't immediately return to the marriage class the second week, or the one after that. Rush and I continue putting pencil marks in the margins of the book. There are wild exclamations when we come across something questionable and tiny stars when something illuminates. Next to this statement there is a check mark, a circle and a tiny star: "I'm going to treat my self-centeredness as the main problem in the marriage."[16]

When I go to class a month later, I go without Rush, aware that a single woman in a marriage class is likely to draw some sympathy. It is week five already, and the class is being taught by a young couple in the church named Dylan and Lisa. The topic is "Loving the Stranger" in marriage and how we find the balance of speaking truth with love.

Lisa says that the best thing you can do in a marriage is talk everything out, even if it means staying at the table or staying up all night. I get the nerve to raise my hand and respond, "I find not talking things out can be a good thing, too. You know, sleeping off the rage. Not everything worth thinking is worth saying." Lisa and Dylan thank me for my comment, and my heart beats loudly from the exposure.

As the summer wanes, every time I show up at Outpost for another class followed by another worship service, I have this uneasy feeling in my belly that I am waiting for something to happen, waiting for someone to do something, anything, that will allow me to trust them. Trust them to do what? I'm not entirely sure, but I'm beginning to suspect trust is mine to give rather than theirs to prove.

⊜ ⊜ ⊜

It *is* a mystery—this church thing that binds me to a perfect Christ and an imperfect people, this marriage thing that binds me to a perfect God and an imperfect man. It is why when Rush asks, "Do you trust me?" I respond with a high-pitched lilt, "No, but I love you."

I insisted on cubic zirconium when Rush I first started talking rings. I was still a senior in college and embarrassed by the flash of fancy things. I wasn't even sure I wanted an engagement ring if he didn't have to wear one too. Rush settled on a simple diamond and platinum band that would serve as both my engagement and wedding ring. My uncle, a jeweler in New York City, said cubic zirconia get cloudy with time.

I wore it on my middle finger. It was too big for my ring finger, even after we paid to have the band taken down a size. Truth be told it was a small pleasure flicking off anyone who grabbed my wrist and shrieked, "Now let me see that sparkler!" As a young bride, I already felt like I was playing dress-up. Once when I slid a pack of gum across the counter at CVS, the clerk took one look at my hand and raised her brow as if she were contemplating calling child services.

We had been married two years and were living in the Bay Area when my grandmother gifted me the purple tanzanite ring she'd culled from a trip to South Africa. "Is it okay if I wear this one for a while?" I asked Rush, breath quick. Although Grannie Annie was almost eighty-five, her gnarled hands had once been lithe, and the ring fell down the shaft of my finger smoothly. It looked like a sun with diamonds shooting out like triangles, or the face of a lion. I got so many compliments on that ring, people oohing and aahing and telling me it looked like Princess Di's. I let them, too.

I liked my new ring so much that when I got off the BART in Oakland after work one afternoon, I wandered down College Avenue to the fancy jewelry shop. "How much would it cost to weld this to a wedding band?" I asked. The rings didn't quite match, the one being thin like a needle, the other thick like a toothpick. When I dropped them off the following day, I told the owner, "I know they don't really go together, but I like them like that." She said they would be beautiful. She was right. The narrowness of the tanzanite ring kept my wedding band firmly in place on my ring finger for the first time since I'd been married. It had never fit so well.

After we moved back to North Carolina for me to attend graduate school, I missed the way Oakland fit, even though it hadn't been a perfect fit either. I missed the crisp weather and the crunchy people. There I had been an explorer, choosing new routes home from work, researching new restaurants online. People were always visiting, in and out, calling us at five in the morning from Yosemite and asking if they could sleep on our futon. The neighbors downstairs wrote us emails letting us know the dog whined while we were at work and my heels were loud on the hardwood floor, but Annie cooked us meat-free meals and Andrew taught Rush how to play the guitar. Michelle from across the hall used to say, "I love people stacked on people. You never feel alone."

I could have been forgiven for wanting a big house or big yard when we moved to more affordable Durham, but all I wanted was a house close enough so the neighbors could hear me scream. By the time all our boxes were unpacked for the third time in two years, the familiar feeling of panic returned. I called my older brother, Charlie, to tell him I was moving back West, this time alone, "so don't get any ideas about leaving."

"Nah, I'll be sticking around Seattle for awhile," he said. "Molly graduates in May. And sh-sh-sh-sheee," he stuttered, drawing out his vowels like the speech therapist taught him. "Sheee already has a teaching job lined up next year."

"I'm serious. I've got one official summer left between this graduate program, and I won't be spending it here."

"It can't be that bad. You've been in Durham, what, three weeks?"

"Want a mental picture? I am sitting on our screened-in back porch right now in head-to-toe REI gear that cinches. It cinches, Charlie, and I'm still getting bit." I lifted up my pant leg to scratch my ankle, and sure enough there was a white, amoeba-like bump pressing to the surface. "I'm just so . . . homesick."

"For Seattle? You've never even lived here."

"I know, but—stop laughing—I'm serious. I keep picturing those lavender cupcakes in Capital Hill and thinking I'm supposed to be there eating one. On a bench. In a raincoat. With Bon Iver playing in the background."

"Is Rush cool with you taking off?"

The truth was I hadn't officially asked him. I hadn't officially asked God either. I'm sure of it because all sorts of wise people like my mother and my spiritual director asked me what God was speaking to me. But it was hard to hear anything under the suffocating cloak of heat. I only knew this: this awful being *here* wasn't working.

≡ ≡ ≡

I've never been entirely sure what people mean by "trust." I asked Rush, "What do you mean when you say you want me to trust you?

Am I trusting that you'll *do* something? Because there have been times when you haven't kept your word. Or am I trusting you to *be* someone? I know you'll fall short. We all do."

He paused. "I think what I'm asking you to do is trust me to be the person you know I *can* be."

This wasn't a satisfactory answer. *Can* was considerably less reliable than *will*. For the first two years of marriage, every time I'd ask Rush to do something and he promised to try, I'd make a stink face. "Try? Why don't you just plan on it?"

It wasn't until I heard Barbara Brown Taylor preach a sermon at Duke Chapel on trust that the word became loosed from its chains. She explained how she used to believe that trust depended foremost on the evidence of trustworthiness. For instance, until a friend proved that she could keep others' secrets, Taylor didn't trust her with her own. The only problem with this logic was that trust always depended on something outside of her control. "It was like my trust was not mine to give," she reflected in her sermon. She went on, "Then one day someone offered me a different definition of trust and it turned my logic inside out. He said, 'Your ability to trust doesn't have anything to do with anyone but you. You weigh the risks and then you decide.' Basically, he said, trust means deciding if you can handle it if you get screwed."[17]

When it comes to trust, it is God who always makes the first move to trust us, Taylor reminded me. In Genesis 15, God appears to Abram and tells him that his descendants will be as numerous as the stars. Abram wants to know how he can be sure this will come to pass. Disappointment wounds even ancient hearts. God responds by asking Abram to set the scene for a covenant ceremony.

A covenant in the Hebrew language was literally understood to be "cut" between two parties, a deathly image for the cut that would occur in the relationship should the promise be broken. Abram prepares the animal sacrifices, cutting them in two and creating an aisle of dead carcasses. As night falls, God puts Abram in a deep sleep and comes

to him in the form of a smoking firepot and a flam
down the aisle of the covenant carcasses. Abram, f
still in a trance. He doesn't even walk down the aisle
in return. God doesn't even ask him to yet.

Surely the evidence was against us when God took that first step
down the aisle. There had been a trip-up in the garden and a murder
in the field and a last-ditch effort to keep the "good ones" alive on a
raft out to sea. At one point in Scripture, we're even told that "the
LORD was sorry that he had made humankind on the earth" (Genesis
6:6). We weren't worthy of trust based on the evidence. But God
weighed the risk of loving us and said, "I can handle it if I get screwed."
And God did. Again and again.

To think, I can *choose* to trust the people I love most? To think,
belonging is something that happens *with* me and not *to* me? On the
one hand, it was a wonderful thought. Trust had always been a test
that someone—Rush, my parents, the church—either passed or failed.
If they failed, I withdrew my affection, as if to say, *You don't deserve me*
or *I didn't really want you anyhow.* If they passed, I was happy, secure,
optimistic, but only until the next test. Trust could be gained or lost
with the changing of the tides, and I was a seasick ragdoll. On the
other hand, if I had some agency in the matter, it meant I'd have to
accept responsibility for things I'd rather not. Things like my spotty
bouts of trust in marriage or my spotty attendance at church.

Accountability has never been my strong suit.

But, hey, I can try.

=13=

Summer schedules make it difficult to find rhythm in Durham. I don't
make it to more than two marriage classes in the end, and Rush and
I finish the book on our own, discussing it in car rides to the mall or
over wine on the back porch. Rush's boss is on sabbatical for a few

months, and I get to fill in once at his church as a guest preacher. There's a trip to Nanny's eightieth birthday party in South Carolina and a flight to San Francisco to visit our niece and her dad. Four days are spent perched in the redwoods of Marin County attending a work retreat, and my ache for home is unbearable as I take the bus from SFO up the 101. It hurts to breathe the piney air.

The retreat is a program of the Center for Courage & Renewal, a nonprofit cofounded by Parker Palmer that helps sustain the leadership of those who serve. What started as an initiative to support the integrity of teachers and sustain them in their demanding roles became salient for other helping professions like doctors and nonprofit leaders, who often feel disillusioned by the disconnect between their profession's values and its day-to-day realities. I began working remotely with the organization while I was in graduate school, helping to develop programs for clergy and congregational leaders, a group that often showed up to retreats like these worn from the pressures of ministry.

We meet in a stucco and stone mansion, completed in 1917 as a bridegroom's present to his bride. While the property has been in use as a retreat center since the death of the bride in the late seventies, a relic of the couple's devotion remains carved into the grounds; a heart-shaped lawn is testament to their extravagant love. Twenty-five of us gather in the parlor each morning as the sun presses its face up against the bay window. We arrange ourselves in a circle of couches and chairs. I am the youngest participant by ten or so years. I haven't yet traded my knee-high boots for clogs or my hammered gold earrings for colored glass ones, but I feel an easy trust with this barefaced bunch.

Our facilitators, Caryl and Faye, lead the group in exploring the interior geography of our lives, a terrain that we travel day in and day out with little reflection. "What is the geography of your soul right now?" Faye asks. Photographs of different geographical terrains are splayed across the room. "Get up. Look around. Let your image find you."

Let your image find you? I know what I'm looking for. Rolling hills are allowable, but there can be no discernible pattern in the ground. No weaving vineyards. No plots of square farm land. No mountains in the distance. No water cutting movement through the earth. Since moving to Durham, I've felt flat as a pond without a plop.

My eyes fix on a black-and-white photo laid out on the windowsill in an adjacent parlor. In it, a man stands with his back to me in a grassy field. His head is tilted slightly to one side, and I can see he is wearing spectacles. A kite flies in an unbroken line from his hand to the sky. I pick up the picture and return to my seat in the circle to study it better.

I quickly identify myself as the kite in the wind. But who is the man flying me? Who is the earth grounding me? I mine the photo for more metaphors, turning the picture clockwise in my lap as if a new orientation might give me a new perspective.

It comes to me. A kite flies best when unobstructed. It flies best when the ground beneath its wings is smooth, steady, predictable. A kite that flies in the mountains only gets tangled up in itself. A kite that flies in the ocean comes dangerously close to drowning, exhausting itself with trying to stay above the waves. But a kite on the flats—in the plains— well, a kite can flourish there. It can come down and take a rest when it gets tired. It can go back up when it's ready for another tousle. Maybe stable ground is the best terrain a kite could want.

It is a paradox of the landscape. To be tethered to the ground both opposes the kite's strength and gives it the lifeline it needs to take risks. Without someone holding it, the kite would be swept away in its own whirlwind.

A revelation, scribbled in my notebook, reads, *The tension is what creates flight.*

ᗧ ᗧ ᗧ

After our visit to the mountains in the early part of summer, I get an email from Jason. Jaylynn has taken a new position with the church conference that frees her up on Sunday mornings. The two no longer have to spend the day apart. Jason writes, "I didn't realize how much I hated being separated until the whole family was going to my church. Suddenly Jaylynn could see things I couldn't, she could greet people I couldn't get to, could notice things I never would. Suddenly parishioners who didn't care for me liked me more because of her."

In *The Meaning of Marriage*, Kathy Keller describes marriage as an embrace of the "other." She writes, "We accept and yet struggle with the gendered 'otherness' of our spouse, and in the process, we grow and flourish in ways otherwise impossible."[18] Like the kite flying high above solid ground, the opposing weight of a partner allows us to move safely and freely. I see this kind of creative tension in more than just a marriage between man and woman or Christ and the church. I see the gift of "otherness" in relationships of love and friendship where we often choose to be with people who complement rather than match our strengths. Most importantly, I see the dance of the "other" in the persons of the Trinity—Father, Son and Spirit—who according to theologian Marguerite Schuster "can't be separated but are rather more themselves because of this relationship."[19] This had been true enough for Jason and Jaylynn.

In graduate school, we learned how to read this "other" charitably, whether it was the pastor in the pulpit or the cynic within ourselves. *Charity* is an ancient word for Christian love, an ancient reminder of love's compassion to the needy in us all. Reading with charity meant not automatically picking the author's idea apart line by line without stepping back and taking the long view. Instead, when we could, we made a choice to trust the best intentions of our brothers and sisters in the tradition (even if that brother was named Tertullian and thinks you, like all women, are the devil's gateway[20]). It's not that we couldn't be critical or disagree with someone. It's that we couldn't be dismissive of someone or some text without struggling on, past the point of comfort, off the cliff of certainty and deep into the waters of our common muck.

One of the touchstones for group work with the Center for Courage & Renewal is "When the going gets rough, turn to wonder." I love this touchstone. Wonder is a powerful anecdote to cynicism. Wonder allows us to marvel at the "otherness" of those who walked before us or sit beside us without trying to make them behave. When we offer charity to the "other"—in ourselves, our marriage, our church—we walk in the way of Jesus who in his own body encountered the strangeness of our humanity and found it worth the risk of love.

Lesson Three

THE DISCIPLINE OF SHOWING UP

Inspiration is for amateurs—the rest of us just show up and get to work.

CHUCK CLOSE

14

American filmmaker Woody Allen famously said, "Showing up is eighty percent of life."[1] I imagine the same is true for going to church. Finding a place to belong seems to depend more on my ability to show up—often and fully—than it does on what happens once I get there. That stuff is important, but that stuff I can't control.

This belief is, in part, what sends me up the stone stairs of Outpost Community Church through the summer and into the fall of my "first third year." However inconsistent I've been, I kept my promise to Bess to give this church a chance. How much of a chance it was, well, that I can't be sure. And so, whether it's due to motivation or momentum, I decide to keep going past the point of feeling and into the realm of habit. By acting as if I believe in the blessing of this community, can I will it to be so?

It isn't enough to flirt with the occasional Sunday activity between trips out of town. If I am really going to belong, I'll need to learn a name or two. I'll need to talk to strangers.

There is something familiar about showing up for worship at Outpost each week. It's like a distant cousin in my Catholic family, the cousin you stumble upon as an adult and find refreshing at first as he spouts new narrations of your past and puts twists on timeless traditions. There is no fount to dip your finger in when you enter his house, nor the smell of incense wafting from the old-fashioned stove, but you nevertheless recognize some customs that put you at ease as you're getting to know him.

It's a soggy autumn morning when I arrive outside of Outpost at 10:53 a.m. with the wetness of morning eyes. After snaking my bike lock around a handicap sign, I raise my face toward the stairs where two ushers in cropped red vests are perched. A young woman with dark hair stands erect on one side of the entryway in a beige dress that swishes when she swivels. On the other side is an older man who looks like he could have roasted a dog with my Grandpa Baa in Grosse Point Shores. I give the man a nod and take a bulletin from the young woman, making firm eye contact like Dad taught me.

The gathering space is a bird's nest of activity, children waddling near their parents' legs, young adults leaning on the announcements table and older folks who have stopped in the middle of the action to look for God knows what in their pocketbooks. I put a dopey smile on my face and move with purpose toward the sanctuary. As I cross the threshold, my feet pressing into velvet carpet the color of wine, I tell myself, *The hardest part is over.*

The pews in the sanctuary form a wooden semicircle, like Noah's ark chopped in two, and I take my place on the left edge of the boat with no species to match but the ability to jump ship quickly if needed. Next begins a series of tactics to buttress myself against small talk. I feel for keys or anything else I can grope under the guise of looking busy. I examine the putt-putt-sized pencil with its putt-putt-sized hole carved out of the pew in front of me. I grab the Bible to see which version is used here. I didn't even know there were different versions— or that the Catholics include additional books in their Bible—until I was in college. These things matter, I'm told.

When it's close to start time, Martin files in the swinging side door of the sanctuary and Bess takes her seat next to him. I wonder if I might sit with her next time but don't know if this is allowed. (She says later that it is, but I've never seen anyone do it, which makes me think it's not.) We hush ourselves, and my eyes scan the sanctuary for people who look like me or don't. I'm not sure which I prefer. At the front are a handful of folks in their late sixties or early seventies. They have kind faces. I expect they were blond at one point. At the back on that same side are young couples, some with babies looking to position themselves for an easy escape and some looking around like me but with shoulders touching. The balcony people aren't even visible from where I sit, but I suspect they might be my kind of people save for the fact that they don't appear to be trying as hard as I am down here on the lower decks. In the middle of the sanctuary are divinity school students looking confident but exhausted. I don't want to sit next to them. I feel squarely in the infinite abyss of adulthood in which there are no longer academic terms to mark the time.

God help us.

As one body we rise to sing the opening songs, a mixture of timeless hymns and contemporary worship tunes. I sing steadily, changing all the he's to her's and changing all the Fathers to Mothers in order to enact a dose of liturgical affirmative action on behalf of the female sex. Sometimes, I even refuse to sing the "female" part that comes second in call-and-response songs. Even though this feels the most trivial of all protests, it keeps me sane. Despite the fact that I'm sure, very sure, God is neither male nor female and that this kind of either-or thinking obscures our worship of a trinitarian God, I sing my transgressions low. It's too soon, I think, to appear a heretic.

When the songs have left our lips, Bess invites us into a time of confession. Here on our knees, we are given a moment of silence to account for the previous week's sins and the persistent ones too, like vanity and jealousy and complaining about perfectly nice people who do perfectly annoying things. We are assured of God's love for us. We are also assured that we are nothing without this love. And while I believe this, I wonder, when in my life have I ever been without God's love? Isn't my very being given by God, stamped with a divine image, born into a history of people who encountered God in the crevices of human life?

Have I ever not belonged to God?

After we stand in assurance that our sins have been removed from us "as far as the east is from the west" (or at least as far as this Sunday to the next), we turn to one another and say, "Peace of Christ." Of course, if you are alone, you wait a beat while the first round of hugs and handshakes are shared between the people who came together, mothers and daughters, husbands and wives, roommates and friends. When it's my turn, I give a firm squeeze to the Dutch-looking man in front of me and say, "Peace be with you," choosing to use the Catholic iteration in an effort to maintain what familiarity I can.

But there is nothing familiar about where this is headed each week. It is not leading to the Eucharist I fought for growing up. It's leading to the sermon, the roughly twenty-five-minute or so explication of this season's theme or topic. Here at Outpost, the Eucharist is offered at the Sunday morning services only once a month.

A symbol of thanksgiving, the Eucharist was practiced by early Christians as an actual meal shared between believers; it wasn't until the second century that it became differentiated as a sacramental meal that priests offered as a sacrifice for the sins of the church. Because of its reconciliatory power, churchgoers sought to receive the sacrament as frequently as possible. But starting as early as the fourth century and lasting through the medieval period, the frequency of the sacrament declined as reverence for the ritual increased. By the Fourth Lateran Council in 1215, the sacramental meal was required only on Easter;[2] it wasn't until the twentieth century that the Catholic Church increased the frequency to every Mass where the faithful were gathered.[3] Protestant Reformers, on the other hand, reacted against excessive devotion to the Eucharist in as much as it came dangerously close to suggesting Christ's accomplishment on the cross needed to be mediated afresh each week. Even so, John Calvin, the founder of Presbyterianism, argued that the Eucharistic meal should be offered "at least once a week" and John Wesley, Methodism's cornerstone, was said to have received the sacrament every four or five days.[4] Neither man would have been satisfied with the infrequency of the ritual in many American Protestant churches today.

When I inquire about why we only celebrate the Eucharist once a month here, a longtime member tells me there was concern that the sermon would have to be cut short. Granted, at an hour and fifteen minutes, the service is already stretching the limits of my Catholic attention span. Still, without the sacrament to guide me, I'm not sure how to prevent this feast of human words from overshadowing a taste of the Word incarnate. It's too easy for me to spend an entire worship service writing things the pastor said on the bulletin followed by a question mark ("Jesus as new sheriff in town?"). What is the point of worship if not to remember that God redeemed ordinary things like bread, wine and meandering sermons? What is the point if not to remember that God was redeeming me?

It turns out even your family can feel like a stranger sometimes.

ᵬ15ᵬ

My grandmother Nanny must have been relieved when I was born. While Dad had lobbied for the name Bernadette and Mom preferred the more lighthearted Kelsey, the two finally agreed to call me Abby. Nanny bristled at the suggestion. She would not have her first grand-daughter share the same first and last name as the nightclub singer of the 1960s deemed "the swingingest sexpot in show business."[5] Instead, I came into this world as Erin, a Gaelic name for peace, a name I've always considered more aspirational than prophetic.

My dad comes from a long line of Irish Catholics, the ones who wail, "Jesus, Mary and Joseph!" when the Michigan Wolverines are down a touchdown, and the ones who still send cards on St. Paddy's Day. The men were often skinny and red-faced from a diet of beer and hot dogs, while the women had what we in the American Midwest call "fannies"—bottoms round enough to open a door with one thrust. I didn't much like the sugared ham and potatoes that were served around the holidays; by the time dinner was ready I had usually gorged myself on the peppermint patties that Nanny put out in a trail of crystal candy dishes. She was always feeding us, wanting us to eat more, apologizing if we said we'd had too much. This is how she fed us tradition too.

Dad was the oldest of five, and he took to the Sunday ritual of attending Mass like syrup on egg toast. He even contemplated a calling to the priesthood but would later say to me with wonder, "I just wasn't all the way there." Not all of the Lane children were as committed. Aunt Trish, the only girl among the clan, routinely went to the local Big Boy to meet friends who *had* attended Mass so she could return home with their bulletins as faulty evidence of her own devotion. It is another mystery of the faith why some children latch on to the rituals and others pull anchor out.

I was initiated into the Church with a capital *C* before I'd met the extended family, so to speak. A baby, I was likely drooling down my virgin-white gown when my parents and godparents promised to raise me in the Christian tradition.

"What name do you give this child?" Father Mitch would have asked, just as he had asked other parents before, just as his own parents were asked.

"Erin Steffen Lane," my parents would have replied as Nanny nodded in approval. My middle name carries her family's legacy. I imagine she does a quick sign of the cross—up, down, left, right.

Clearing his throat of coffee breath, a donut crumb perhaps still lingering on his mouth, Father Mitch would continue, "It will be your duty to bring her up in keeping with God's commandments as Christ taught us."

Although I understand nothing, my parents stand in on my behalf and enact my initiation. My godparents—a friend of my mother's we mysteriously call Aunt Sparky and my dad's bachelor brother, Uncle Tim—agree to help, although neither commit to anything specific, and thus are poised to become only the occasional backyard barbeque and wedding guests. The baptism is sealed by the harried hands of Father Mitch, which dip into the bowl of holy water and trace the cross over my forehead.

This is as small as I'll ever be.

Baptism is a sacrament in the Catholic Church, a practice instituted by Christ and entrusted to the people to perform in his absence. Like Christ—who Christians believe was God in the flesh—baptism is a sign of God's commitment to be known through the ordinary elements of water, oil and human bodies. In other Christian traditions, baptism takes place when the individual is older, presumably with more choice. But I've always thought the baptism of infants is the more humane route; much how piercing a baby's ears might seem like child abuse at first but is ultimately saving that baby from a painful trip to Claire's down the road. Maybe it's best some of us have our baptism chosen for us. We are handed a tradition, betrothed to that tradition, written into the history of that tradition. Whether we resist or not, a whole community of faith has promised to pray that our faith will take root. A human life, a single name, becomes sanctified, made holy, set apart through no effort of our own.

The sacraments do this kind of thing, help us to see ourselves more clearly, our small and precious place in God's kin-dom. According to Orthodox theologian Alexander Schmemann, the sacraments are not "an escape from the world" but rather "a vantage point from which we can see more deeply into the reality of the world."[6] In baptism, we hear God's reality for our lives spoken over us, just as it was spoken over Jesus after his baptism, "You are my child, my beloved; with you I am well-pleased" (see Mark 1:11). God says to each of us, "You are mine. You are loved. You are worthy."

Didn't you know?

The gift of belonging is already ours. We're "preapproved," as writer Anne Lamott is fond of saying. The question is not, Can we belong? The question is, Will we belong? Will we make real the words of baptism by responding as if they were true? This was my God. These were my people. It was them I'd belong to or them I'd reject, but the one, holy, catholic and apostolic church was with whom my lot was cast. I didn't know another way, didn't know how it would have turned out if I'd found God at a Young Life camp fifteen years ago like my best friend Caroline or through the Jesus movement that washed over the country fifty years ago like Martin. God was family, and we blessed God's family and ours in prayers that ended, "In the name of the Father, Son and Holy Spirit, amen."

Dad's was a faith that was never unwound from family, never left up to choice. Going to church on Sundays was what good, well-behaved children did, along with sending handwritten thank-you notes and brushing your teeth before bed. It was also, Dad told us, what Catholics did if we wanted to avoid the divine stink eye. We never got to skip Mass because we didn't feel like going or we wanted to sleep in or we might miss the tailgate at Milwaukee County Stadium. Even when we traveled together, Dad would open the drawer that separated our hotel beds, pushing the King James Bible aside and pulling out the worn-thin pages of the phonebook to check when Mass was being held nearby. Charlie and I traded frowns whenever he settled on a time. What did he think was going to happen if we missed church just this once? I sort of pitied him his superstition along with his dandruff and creeping psoriasis.

But I'm thankful Dad didn't let up. I'm thankful that he was relentless in dragging us to the foot of the altar with our kid arms cupped in front of our kid chests to commune with the body of Christ like it was just what our people did. It took the guesswork out of it all, the what ifs, the guilt trips of should we or shouldn't we, because we always should, even if the only Mass we could get to was in Spanish. We didn't have to be on time or comb our perm, as long as we received Communion and sang every last word of the closing hymn. We showed up, expecting God would too, even if it didn't always seem like God was there.

= 16 =

I am a person who needs rhythm. I need to wake up with a plan, even if that plan is to have no plan between the hours of 9:00 and noon. It needs to be decided beforehand, in some saner moment when I am not so attached to morning mood (and the uneasy feeling of having swallowed a tooth somewhere around 3:00 a.m.). *What is a good use of time on the sabbath day?* I wonder. Is it sloth or rest to watch three consecutive episodes of *The Good Wife* before showering? Is it discipline or perfectionism to tinker on the opening paragraph of a blog post while the dog skulks near the door? Is it "good boundaries" or "bad social skills" to decline an invitation to dinner in favor of a box of Annie's mac and cheese at 4:30 p.m.? The possibility that I will choose unwisely is enough to keep me in bed all day with my imaginary abscess.

When Rush is gone on Sundays, I parcel out time like an old person sorts pills. There's the Sunday morning apportionment (something churchy), the noontime booster (something social) and a collection of evening supplements (something creative) to keep me thrumming throughout the day. Of course, there's no guarantee I'll stick to the script. Sometimes my fingers are too stiff to pry open my morning dose of prayer, and sometimes I forget to take my pre-scription for an afternoon walk. That's when I need a companion who still has her wits about her to say, "Remember what's good for you, old fool."

This particular Sunday I call on Juli and Corey to look after me. They're still searching for a church home, and I could use some re-inforcements in the pew. I shuffle quietly around the house, following my morning routine of Fiber One and an episode of *House Hunters* until it's time to leave, but despite careful planning to the contrary, I arrive at church early and am too wimpy to save seats. When the service is over, I flatten my body against the pew and "excuse me, thank you" my way down the aisle to meet them.

"Hey, guys. I, uh, was planning on trying out the young adults' luncheon today. What do you think?"

Juli glances over at Corey, who's talking to a friend from school he ran into. "I'm not sure about him. I think he's feeling a little exhausted today."

I spurt out "I get it" before my disappointment registers. A new, more nebulous plan for the afternoon is beginning to form now. I reason with myself about the merits of a quiet afternoon spent in socks. Maybe I'll even curl up in front of the window with my Bible. More likely I'll stop by the Redbox machine on my bike home and rent that new Woody Allen movie Rush refuses to watch.

When Corey finally turns toward Juli and me, he reaches out his long arm to grab my shoulder. "Hey, friend. Delightful to see you."

"You too, buddy. Just *delightful*," I mimic his southern vernacular. "Juli was saying you may not be up for lunch today?"

He scrunches his face, "I'd normally be game. But I'd just rather spend time with you than a bunch of strangers."

I get it. Of course I do. So it is as if I am reasoning with myself when I ask Corey, "But isn't that what Sunday is for? Aren't we supposed to be hanging out with a bunch of strangers?"

⊟ ⊟ ⊟

I've been reading a lot about strangers lately from Parker Palmer. Parker grew up in the Chicago suburbs, like me, only in the 1940s. He was white and male so, naturally, was told that he would become a great success. He attended a prestigious liberal arts college, tried a year of seminary and finally decided to pursue a doctorate in the sociology of religion. By everyone's estimation, he was on track to become a university president. Instead, he moved to D.C. and began work as a community organizer and adjunct professor. After five years, he was burnt out and in need of a new rhythm.

Along with his family, he decided to take a year sabbatical and move to a Quaker learning community outside of Philadelphia called Pendle Hill. He and the busboy would make exactly the same amount of yearly pay and share many of the same responsibilities. Despite advice from colleagues that he was committing career suicide, he continued on at Pendle Hill for eleven years, where he served as student, dean, teacher and writer in residence until 1985. It was here that he wrote a book called *The Company of Strangers: Christians and the Renewal of America's Public Life,* a sort of treatise against the retreat to the comfort and safety of the home that characterized the 1980s but had begun decades earlier in the aftermath of World War II. In it, Palmer calls on Christians to reclaim our vocation to live amongst strangers, writing, "As our privacy deepens and our distance from the public increases, we pay a terrible price. We lose our sense of relatedness to those strangers with whom we must share the earth; we lose our sense of comfort and at-homeness in the world."[7]

In the United States, we've seen increasing privatization of what used to be social spaces held in common, like schools and prisons. What does this mean for the church? It means that along with the DMV, it's one of the few public spaces left where we can regularly come into contact with people we wouldn't choose. While there is some import to gathering with like-minded believers—for instance, the black church has historically been an affinity space for political organizing and social support[8]—in many churches the lack of noticeable diversity is sad. The same segregation of special interests we see in the political arena threatens to taint the waters of our baptismal founts. Our churches are becoming like our media—one audience for you, fiery Fox News, and one for you, dear Daily Show. We wouldn't be caught dead sitting through a thirty-minute program, let alone an hour-long worship service, that espoused views contrary to our own.

Globalization, a big word used to describe the reality of a worldwide marketplace, has both increased the possibility of our connectivity and decreased the feeling that our contributions are making a difference. In turn, many of us have grown indifferent to what happens in our public spaces, focusing on the only world we can control, a world much smaller than the one we actually live in. Pope Francis has referred to this phenomenon as the "globalization of indifference." He says, "The culture of comfort, which makes us think only of ourselves, makes us insensitive to the cries of other people, makes us live in soap bubbles which, however lovely, are insubstantial; they offer a fleeting and empty illusion which results in indifference to others."[9] But we're not just indifferent to others; globalization has also made us ignorant of others as we increasingly become removed from those people who don't look and talk and think like us. It's no wonder I can't think of a single young Republican in Durham I could invite to dinner.

There's a series of parables in the fourteenth chapter of Luke's Gospel in which Jesus talks dinner etiquette while sharing a sabbath meal at one of the Pharisees' house. Now if you grew up in Sunday school, you'll probably remember the Pharisees as "the teacher's pets" who were always trying to find favor with God through dogged obedience to religious law. It's easy for me to think of this group as a symbol for why organized religion is oppressive: it's a group of fanatics who can't let go of their "traditional" values to see how the living God is moving here and now. Modern critiques of the church—that it's judgmental, sheltered, sexist[10]—could have easily been targeted at these rabbinical scholars. I'm tempted to place myself outside of their ranks. But Jesus spends a lot of time with the Pharisees, and I should be grateful for that. I suspect this is a group of people to which I would have belonged, albeit reluctantly.

As the story begins, I imagine Jesus and the Pharisees sitting outside on the pre-modern equivalent of a screened-in porch, drinking sweet tea with stiff lips, when they're interrupted by a strange commotion—a man with a swollen body. Maybe he's begging, maybe he's just loitering a little too close, but Jesus asks everyone if it's okay if he just goes ahead and heals the man even though it's the sabbath, a holy day set aside from toil. An uncomfortable intrusion to an intimate gathering, the event stuns the Pharisees into silence, so Jesus tells a few stories about table manners to rouse them.

The first story is about seating arrangements. Instead of vying for prime real estate (think middle of the table between two people you like), take your seat at the least important place (think end of the table where you'll be cornered by a twenty-something intern who works on Capitol Hill). The next parable is about invitations. Don't hand them out to the people you adore (like those friends from college) or the ones who make you look cool (like those neighbors with the worm composter) but invite the poor and sick and lame. And just in case you were about to say something glib like, "Aren't we all poor in spirit?" Jesus' last illustration gives instruction about how precisely to find the poor, sick and lame among us. He's not talking about inviting your Aunt Martha over for dinner with her bum hip, although I don't think he'd object. No, he's a little more specific here that the people most likely to be breaking bread with God are found sitting on busy sidewalks and hidden side streets, the highway off-ramps and the darkened alleys. These are the people most likely to show up to the sabbath party while the rest of us are sitting at home collecting excuses.

"Urge people to come in so that my house will be filled" (Luke 14:23 CEB), the host in the parable begs, and I can't help but think of God as an earnest party planner, perched near the window with a glass of wine, bouncing a leg up and down to pass the time, hoping people show up for the revelry. The Costco run has been made, the mini quiches are in the oven, and the napkins that say, "Why do dishes when you can do daiquiris?" are perfectly askew on the coffee table. It'd be sad, pitiful really, if no one got to enjoy the creativity of every detail. And do you want to know who always arrives first? The ones who don't have prior plans. The ones who aren't trying to make it to three different engagements in one night. The ones who shot their grocery money for the month and are somehow able to turn a table of appetizers into a full-blown meal. It's with these people that I want to feel at-homeness. It's in this house that I want to belong. Even if most days I, like Corey, tend to spend parties talking with people I know.

Strangers who are poor, sick and lame wake us up to our need. They live with "less padding between them and the raw forces of life," according to Flannery O'Connor.[11] They challenge our culturally shaped rhythms and subvert our socially acceptable excuses. My pastor friend Jason once asked me, "But don't you think the point of church is to turn strangers into friends?" Heavens no. God's house is big, and our capacity for intimacy with those in it is limited. Besides, I need some strangers to remain strangers this side of life so I don't get too satisfied with my puffed-up version of reality, my small-minded way of doing things, the rituals that have become the right way because they're the only way I've known. More importantly, I need strangers to remain strangers because, in many ways, God remains a stranger to me.

For all the gifts that strands of Christianity like evangelicalism have brought me in the idea of God as daily conversation partner, I also heed the gifts of my Catholic upbringing that remind me God is mystery, maker and host. Recognizing that God is both friend *and* stranger helps me hold the paradox that God is both knowable and unknowable. This is the paradoxical mission of the church, to comfort *and* disrupt, to give rest *and* rile up, to make us feel known *and* make us feel small in the wake of what we cannot know.

Sabbath freedom is not the freedom to spend our time wisely. Instead, sabbath freedom is the freedom to live large. To live large on the sabbath day means choosing to live larger than our own rhythm. When so much of modern life is spent crafting our home, filling it with belongings and guarding it from interruption, going to church is a countercultural practice. Going to church teaches us how to craft a home for the world.

17

Growing up, my world was full of strangers. They blew through our lives like leaves, dropping in unexpectedly, rustling around our ankles and flitting out again through the garage when somebody left the door open. Both parents worked, and caregivers came in and out of our home frequently; first there was Martha, then Alicia, then Jenny with the Wilson Phillips cassette tape. When we moved to a rental house after the divorce, Perk took in a foreign exchange student named Anya who smelled like cooked lamb and told us about partying on the Berlin Wall. Later, Perk even let Dad's sister, Aunt Trish, move into our basement between finishing a degree in nursing and finding a job. The whole family marveled.

Perk was always listening for the voice of God to tell her which stranger to help next. We'd be coming out of the grocery store and she'd see an old woman waiting for the bus and say, "Hold on, kids. I got a word from God. That lady needs a ride."

"That's why she's standing at the bus stop," we'd whine, but sure enough the woman would agree and whoever had called shotgun would be bumped to the back. It was annoying, sure, but thrilling too, to think that the Spirit of God was riding passenger with us. She was good at asking strangers for help too. "Hey, Tall Man, can you help me get this box off the shelf?" she'd ask at the hardware store or "You don't say! I could use an old mattress if you're giving one away." A single mom hadn't the luxury of an illusion like self-reliance.

Strangers didn't always feel like gifts in my life. I resented that we had to rely on them as much as we did. After the divorce, when Charlie and I began flying as unaccompanied minors between Chicago and Detroit, we hit a patch of bad weather and were grounded for the night in Cleveland. The flight attendants were only responsible for getting us to and from the gate. At eight and ten, we were responsible for getting ourselves to the hotel and back again for the first flight out in the morning. I called Perk collect from a payphone. "It's going to be okay, Miss E. Look around the gate area, okay? Find the nicest, most normal looking woman and ask her to look out for you." We spent the night alone, jumping between beds and watching cartoons, but a kind Midwestern woman made sure we woke up on time the next morning and knew which van to take back to the terminal. Charlie and I learned early that we needed strangers to survive, whether we liked them or not. Mostly they scared the bejesus out of me.

I was eight years old when a stranger exposed himself to me in a South Carolina shoe store. Nanny was watching Charlie and me for the afternoon while my parents, just months before they announced their split, went to Savannah to tour plantation homes. I was sitting cross-legged on the far aisle where the kid shoes were lined up, trying to unbuckle a pair of white patent-leather Mary Janes when he approached me from behind and asked if I knew where the men's shoes were. I knew about "stranger danger" like all children of the eighties. No taking candy from strange men in white vans. No trotting off with strange women who claimed they'd been sent to collect us. But these rules conflicted with a Midwestern upbringing that taught us to be friendly above all else. I twisted my head around to answer the stranger's question—"Um, I think they're . . ." It took my eyes a few blinks to focus on what was happening. I didn't know what to do. I always imagined I would do something brave in a moment like that. Sometimes when I tell the story now, I say I took the Mary Jane in my hand and whacked him a good one before running off, but I can't be sure that's true. I know I left the Mary Janes in the middle of the aisle. I know I ran through the store looking for Charlie. I know I put my face against his ten-year-old chest when I found him. "Let's find Nanny," he said to me. The three of us waited outside for the police to take my report. I know the store owner offered me a piece of Trident original-flavored gum.

I developed a coping mechanism for overcoming my fear of strangers. I'd learned it from a dream psychologist years earlier after seeing *Snow White* on the big screen and returning home with nightmares of the evil queen. My parents tried letting me sleep with them for awhile and then, when that got tiring, tried giving me five bucks to ride it out on my own. Nothing worked until I ended up in the very white, very clinical office of a man who told me the next time I met the evil queen in my dream, I should introduce myself to her. Introduce myself to her? "Yes," he said, "The moment you realize you don't have to be scared, just stick out your hand and say, 'Hi. I'm Erin. What's your name?'"

I tried this on adults as I got older. Whether in the "casual carpool" line in Oakland or walking alone in downtown Durham, anytime I felt my chest tightening with fear, I'd stick out my hand, look a stranger in the eye and hope to see something human in us both.

≡18≡

Perk doesn't go to Mass anymore; it isn't personal enough, she says. She doesn't go to the nondenominational church she went to after I left for college either; "I never saw people outside of church." Now, after "God and I talked," she says, she's at a little Presbyterian church down the road where she likes the pastor and the locals too. One Sunday evening, when I have an hour to spare between yet another episode of *House Hunters* and Rush's return home from work, I call her to see how things are going. She never disappoints.

"Hi Perk. What's up?"

"Is everything okay?"

"Yeah, Mom. I just called to see what you were up to."

"Oh, well, can I call you back in five minutes? I'm in the nursery at work."

"Yeah, sure."

Five minutes later the phone rings. "Hi honey, fire away."

"No, Mom. Tell me about you."

"Oh, aren't you nice? Well, today, let's see . . ."

She starts telling me this story about how she thought she was signed up to be the liturgist. My mom is a fantastic liturgist. She really gets the intonation of the whole Scripture-reading thing, her voice falling and rising like the breath of God or a doughy biscuit. The compliments always pour in after she's been up at the lectern, and even though I think she's bragging when she lists them all to me, I would brag too, if I were that good.

Anyway, she wasn't in charge of the liturgy this morning. She was in charge of "fellowship"; at least, that's what the schedule said when she looked at it yesterday. And she doesn't know what *fellowship* really means because she came to Christ when she was in her thirties and didn't grow up with that church lingo. So she calls the church office—instead of Googling it like I would—and a woman gives her a more succinct answer than Google ever could.

"Fellowship equals cookies."

"How do you mean?" my mother presses.

"Cookies. All you need to do is bake cookies and stand by them after the service. That's fellowship."

"How many cookies?"

"Oh, not that many. Four or five dozen."

Perk realizes that this is a big job for a single, sixty-one-year-old woman to handle so she begins to devise a game plan. She can't possibly make it to work on time if she has to stand and make nice at fellowship hour, so she calls her unit to request an EA, or "excused absence," from the first four hours of her shift. They give it to her.

She begins to bake: chocolate chip cookies, sugar cookies, two different kinds of brownies. "I hate when they bring in that store-bought stuff. It just doesn't feel right. It doesn't feel like fellowship," she tells me over the phone. Now she knows what fellowship means, and she's latched on. She even tells me she had to buy new baking sheets, "Because you know those old ones that always stick out the end of the oven so the door won't close? Well, those just won't do."

It sounds really superficial at first, that fellowship equals cookies. Where's Christ in the cookie? an evangelical might ask. Are you sure you don't mean a wafer? a Catholic would insist. But no. Fellowship equals offering. And Perk gets it. I think she always has.

This is the body broken for you. These are the cookies baked for you.

Since showing up at Outpost, I've been invited to more meals than I have the stomach for. And while these meals might seem easy enough for one to provide, I discover they are full of adult food, the kind you need actual recipes for like Mexican lasagna and banana pudding. I even spot a napkin-rimmed basket of molasses cookies at the young-adult luncheon I eventually make it to.

"You know what you should do?" Perk asks me over the phone. I've told her about all the fellowshiping I have been doing lately, wondering what would come of it, hoping it was helping, tiring of the trying.

"You should sign up to be a greeter," Perk offers. "You'll learn names and look busy doing it."

Bess emails a few weeks later asking if I can help collect money at small group dinners on Wednesday nights. It requires me to show up one more day a week than usual, and I secretly suspect this is her plan; any church person worth her salt knows that giving a person a task is the quickest way to cementing her commitment. Keen on her ways, I accept the invitation.

I ask her if I can be in charge of nametags, too.

≈ 19 ≈

I had a mild panic attack going into work each day as a twenty-four-year-old book publicist in San Francisco. I buttoned my slacks and slurped my cereal and walked to the carpool line beneath the freeway.

Our first apartment wasn't readily near the BART train, and the bus ride over the Bay Bridge in stop-and-go traffic made me sick when I first went in for my interview.

Called "casual carpool," a line of pedestrians formed under the freeway to meet a line of cars weaving their way through the parking lot. The system was one of mutual benefits. The pedestrian commuters got a free ride into the city and the car commuters could take the carpool lane, which, at the time, also gave them a free ride into the city. There were pick-up points all over the East Bay, but the agreement—so said my new colleagues and an ill-formatted website—was that all passengers were to be dropped off in the financial district downtown.

We all had our strategies for which cars we got into and which we passed on. It was at the passenger's discretion who to ride with. Sometimes I would let the person behind me cut in line if the car waiting for me to jump in (a) was a two-seater, (b) had two people in it who arrived together or (c) looked beat up. I felt bad about this last one, but I couldn't stomach any more anxiety than the low-level hum to which I had grown accustomed. My ideal candidate for carpool was a Subaru or Prius, preferably driven by a woman, and preferably one that played NPR the whole ride in to prevent any phony small talk. The passenger dictated who to ride with. The driver dictated the interaction.

From the corner of Fremont and Market, where I got dropped off, it was a twenty-minute walk to my office in the Tenderloin District. On my first morning into work, I walked a couple of blocks behind a woman with fire-engine-red hair until she suddenly decided she had to pee. On a Nordstrom storefront. Standing up. My colleagues told stories about how the line for the methadone clinic used to start right outside of our office. People weaning off heroin weren't always the most gracious. Once, an editorial assistant was hit with projectile vomit on her way into work and promptly returned home to take a mental-health day.

My first few months on the job, I often broke into tears for no good reason. My editor stopped by my cubicle during one of the episodes. "I'll come back later," she said kindly. Other times, I tried to melt down in more private spaces, rushing to the bathroom only to find another colleague who assured me, "You'll learn to love it here." "I think I miss my mom," I confessed, and she said, "I do too, sometimes." I had trouble making friends at work. I was never one for socializing "around the water cooler," preferring instead to eat lunch at my desk while trolling online sales. The first boss I ever had said his only complaint about me was that I needed to "loosen up" at work. Apparently, I am bad at being casual, in carpools and in life.

I had been working at the publishing house for less than six months when a request came over the company-wide Listserv. Our office manager was looking for someone to clean out the fifth- and sixth-floor refrigerators every other week. The last woman had quit, fed up with one too many lashings for throwing away someone's stinky cheese or wheat-grass smoothie. The job paid fifty dollars each month. If I stuck with it a year, I'd make six hundred dollars, enough to cover two tickets home for Christmas. When I emailed Steve to accept the gig, he asked, "Are you sure? People get cranky around here about food. I'd hate for you to start off on the wrong foot." Better the wrong foot than no foot, I thought to myself.

"Can I put up a quippy sign or two to keep people in line?" I asked.

"Anything," he replied.

I became a superstar overnight.

It's no exaggeration. What started out as a few signs that said, "Don't be that guy—label or lose it," turned into a biweekly email reminder of farcical proportions. A midsummer email with the subject line "Summer Scrubbin'" started,

Summer Scrubbin'.
Had me a blast.
Summer Scrubbin'.

Happened so fast.
Met a sandwich, crazy with mold.
Met some sushi that smelled so bold.
Summer days drifting away.
To, uh oh, those 'fridger fights.

I never once got in a fight with anyone, and I was merciless—throwing away Tupperware that was buckling at the lip or take-out turned lavender. Our associate publisher stopped a meeting once as I was walking by to tell me that mine were the only emails he wanted to open each week. Another colleague asked me if I'd ever consider publishing my emails in one of those books for the commode.

The strangest part of the whole gig, a job I kept until I left the company after two years, was that almost everybody in the office knew my name. I'd often be waiting for the elevator, staring at the ground, when another colleague would sidle up next to me.

"Hi," I'd say.

"Hi," they'd say back.

"Erin," I offered.

They'd look at me, slowly, before raising their eyebrows in anticipation. "Erin Beam?"

I'd nod.

"I'm a huge fan of your emails."

"Thanks," I'd mumble as we stepped onto the elevator.

Then seven seconds of sheer silence. Followed by an apology.

"I'm funnier in writing."

That gig saved me.

There's a dispute over whether to use plastic or real utensils at the first Wednesday night small group dinner at Outpost, and I stay out of it. I have a job to do. Bess helps me find some blank labels in a chest of drawers near the fellowship hall, and I scrounge up some markers. The money box is all that separates me from the flood of people that pour in when 5:30 hits.

"Hi, I'm Erin," I say, chipper.

"Erin the preschool director?" they ask.

"Nope, Erin Lane," I say. "Can I get you a name tag?"

They shake their heads and laugh, "Everybody knows us here."

"I don't," I reply.

My favorite interaction is when a middle-aged man named Price writes his name all big and loopy over two labels. When he peels one off to put on his sweater, his name is truncated. "Ha, ha," I chuckle like an amused four-year-old. "Half price."

⊟ ⊟ ⊟

Anthropologists have long studied the power of names. In parts of rural Hong Kong, for instance, male villagers must have at least two names to attain adult status; the more names one has the more socialized one is thought to be. Female villagers, on the other hand, lose their name when they marry and later are called by indistinct terms such as "old woman."[12] Throughout history, names have marked such realities as one's divine calling, clan affiliation or self-concept. Plato argued that "everything has a right name for itself," while Socrates pointed out that not everyone has the right to name himself.[13] Names are not entirely our own.

I filed papers for a name change soon after we moved to Durham. "Are you sure you're okay with this?" I had asked Rush ten times already, but he was un-angsty about the whole thing. "I don't know why it used to matter so much to me," he said.

Everyone looked like an off-brand version of themselves at the Durham County Courthouse. Suit sets were wrinkled and ill-fitting, faces the same. People walked around with their eyes fixed straight as if to say, "It is too tiring to deal with your humanity today." I don't suppose a lot of good news is celebrated here; when I inquired about the proper forms for a legal name change, the woman at the desk asked, "Divorce or death?"

"Neither," I replied. "Feminism."

"What's that?"

"I'm still married," I assured her. "I just don't feel like myself."

"Good Lord," she sighed.

My new friends were equally worried about my sudden streak of independence. When I told them I was planning to move to Seattle the following summer, many wondered if I was insane or just insensitive. Whitney said, "I just don't know how you can do it. John and I have never spent a day apart."

"You're not unhappy, are you?" another pressed as we weaved around the perimeter of the mall. "I only ask because Emily thought maybe you and Rush weren't doing well. I told her you were fine. You're fine, right?"

As a pastor's wife, I'd always gained entry into a church's inner circle by virtue of my name. There was instant recognition when I'd introduce myself to someone. "Oh, you're Rush's wife!" they'd say, grabbing my shoulder as if we were old friends. "We love Rush around here." I'd fold my arms into my chest and nod, "I like that guy, too." There were welcome lunches and late-night cookouts and invitations to have dinner at the pastor's house, and I would put on flats and wear my high-waist jeans for coverage.

Now, most Sundays at Outpost, I sit alone. It's my choice, really. I've started going to the early service, the one that starts at 8:30 a.m. and isn't really popular with people my age. Sometimes I sit behind a blond family and pretend that I'm one of them. Once, when only the dad is there, I ask him after the service, "Where is everybody?" He looks at me, perplexed. "There are only five of us." That seems like a lot considering there's only one of me, I think.

I suppose most people who meet me at Outpost think I'm single, and I don't make a point to correct them, even though a woman without a man feels like something of a liability around here. In one sermon alone I note that in all the illustrations women are nagging mothers, hopeful girlfriends or dutiful wives. During another, men are the only examples held to light. A male-driven sports metaphor carries the message. A male-driven exegesis explains how in ancient Judaism circumcision was the mark of *our* faithfulness, never mind that *we* don't all qualify for said procedure. Oh, and God is always a *he*.

It isn't just our names that matter. Our names for God matter too. They mediate the reality of how and to whom we belong. Take, for instance, the name Father. Father, or *Abba*, was the primary name Jesus used to address God throughout the New Testament, even though orthodox Christianity also asserts that Jesus *was* God. Used to affirm the kinship relationship between the distinct "persons" of the Trinity, Father is an important (and surprising) name for the Christian God. However, used to deify the love of human fathers toward their human families is a dangerous and decidedly un-Christian move. Theologian Janet Soskice reminds us, "Jesus's address of God as 'Father' [would have] seemed to the early theologians startling and new. We are jaded now by sloppy eighteenth-century rhetoric of the 'fatherhood of God and the brotherhood of man'; a noble aspiration perhaps, but not the New Testament message."[14] When Christians divorce an understanding of father language from a Trinitarian theology, "Father God" becomes a name that glorifies human masculinity rather than divine intimacy. I know I'm not the only one who has seen this sap seep into Sunday morning worship as men and women are encouraged to heal their "father wounds" in order to renew their relationship with their "heavenly Father." As Americans find themselves entrenched in a "fatherless epidemic," these efforts can appear to be well-meaning attempts to restore the integrity of men. In reality, they make idols out of men and men like gods.

I believe in the creeds, in tradition, in doctrinal history. I'm a baptized Catholic, mind you. But just as our forefathers and foremothers did, I'm tasked with improvising theologies, not just memorizing marching orders. While I'm not interested in throwing out the sacred language of our Scripture—it represents for me a necessary marker of God's presence throughout history—I do think we need to be more creative in coming up with titles for God in worship that could serve the same purpose "Father" does: to convey the surprising and radical invitation for us all to belong to a God of relationship.

No one pronoun is going to be suitable for God, because no one name—even "Father"—can fully grasp who God is. All names necessarily domesticate God. Second-century church thinker Clement of Alexandria articulated this same point, arguing for a multiplicity of names like Father, Creator and God. He wrote, "Taken individually none of these names is expressive of God, but taken together they collectively point to the power of the Almighty."[15] In the same way, taken together, we collectively point to the power of the church.

None of us is meant to have only one name.

We are made whole by the names we collect.

⊟ ⊟ ⊟

I'm beginning to develop a short list of disagreements with the language at Outpost, and I don't know quite what to do with it. I don't want to hold on to it too tightly, letting my cynicism take me out of the action. But I don't want to ignore it either and snuff out a viewpoint that might strengthen this church—and me.

I am pondering this question of if and when to share my thoughts with Martin as Bess and I are coming out of church together one morning. It is one of the great things about Outpost that you can't venture far from it without smelling the aroma of food from Vietnam, Mexico, Polynesia. You might also pass the overweight fiddler outside of the bookshop or the homeless transvestite who promises you he just has one question. These people are part of the neighborhood's gifts.

We're meeting Heather, another young woman in the church, at a sandwich shop. Bess and I order huge Diet Cokes.

"Doesn't it drive you a little mad?" I ask them as I fish my lips against the straw. "All the male imagery? How do you decide when to say something?"

I can tell Heather is no-nonsense. Her job with a large, Christian organization often takes her to places around the world where she is the only woman in the room.

"I know personally I would want to be invested before I started offering criticism," Heather responds. "It matters a lot if you can say, 'I'm in this with you and that's why this is so important to me.'"

I'm in this with you. As I ride my bike home from lunch, the phrase turns over and over again in my head like a wound-up cassette tape. I can't honestly say that yet. I can't say that I have the best interests of the community at heart when I hardly know the community, can I? Martin had said in our first marriage class, "No matter how long you date, how well you know someone, there will always be surprises in the future. Love is about learning how to love the person you discover you're married to down the road."

I suppose this was true enough for the church, too. You can't know what you're getting into when you choose a church, because it's going to change. The pastor you adore will take a job elsewhere. The friend you always sit next to will get divorced and stop coming for a while. The music you hate will become outdated in five years and soon all worship songs will sound like a Mumford and Sons revival (fingers crossed). Sometimes it's a relief to know that your church, your marriage, is going to change.

You will change too.

= 21 =

Fall in the Pacific Northwest is piercing in its perfection. For a few short months the rain stops and the sun is high, and everyone comes out to play—jumping off the diving board at Madison Park Beach, riding motorcycles around Mercer Island, kayaking across Puget Sound. I take a ferry from Seattle to Bainbridge Island, like I've done many times before, but this time it's to attend the first in a series of three retreats that will prepare me to not just work for the Center for Courage & Renewal but to lead their programs as a facilitator. I keep to myself on the ride over, looking out the window to avoid running into other participants prematurely. We will be "on island" together for five days, and I don't want to talk myself out before it's even started.

When we get off the boat on the other side, I take my time approaching the flagpole where we've agreed to meet. A couple of middle-aged women are standing there, including Robin, the registrar at the Center. "Erin, I didn't even recognize with you that short hair!" she marvels when she sees me. "You're always changing it up, aren't you?"

The retreat is designed as a time of mutual discernment for both the participant and the leadership team to make sure the two-year program is a good fit. We spend the first couple of days reflecting together on where we find ourselves in this season of life, aided by the use of poetry and other art forms that, in the words of Emily Dickinson, "tell all the truth but tell it slant."[16]

It's good to spend time with people who seem more enamored with asking life's big questions than trying to solve them. While there's a time and space for such diagnostic work, on these retreats we focus on asking questions of ourselves and each other that are what we call "open and honest." Open and honest questions are questions we can't possibly know the answer to before asking; they help us approach life's unknowns with humility and curiosity. At dinner, I gum strawberries next to Ted, who's just attended a theater workshop on improvisational comedy. "Most questions that come up in a scene can apply to life in general," he tells me. "What comes next? What can I offer? What makes this relationship matter?" Little questions are welcome here, too, like when the chocolate torte comes out of the kitchen, and I ask Ted, "What makes someone a sugar addict?" I honestly don't know.

It's a phrase from a William Stafford poem on day two that acts as a clarion. The poem is called "The Gift" and reflects on the terrain we miss noticing each day as we shuffle around with heads down and lists bulleted. We keep our world small this way, small and squirrel-like. Stafford invites us to venture into a different country. It's a terrain found outside our office window, in the handiwork of our grand-mother's quilts, between the notes of a song. It's a terrain found, Stafford writes, "after the sermon."[17]

Not in the sermon. Not during the sermon. After the sermon. I circle it once. Then twice. In my fixation on the sermons at Outpost, I've somehow made them into the focal point I'm so stubbornly against. Surely there is a different country I haven't visited at Outpost yet, a different reality that I might notice if only I could learn to linger.

22

I accept a good number of invitations to get to know people my first few months at Outpost. My strategy is to say yes to any opportunity to eat, drink or greet that comes my way in an effort to bypass the awkwardness of another stranger asking me if I am a student and my responding with, "Nope. Just a regular adult."

Soon, I start extending invitations of my own.

I think of these invitations as tiny muscle flexers in sociability, nec-essary if I don't want to remain a skinny-fat congregant, the kind who looks spiritually healthy from a distance but who is flabby in her faith once you start to poke the surface. Perhaps my vocation as a writer has given me some insight into the power of small steps—small steps that don't depend on inspiration, baby words that one day bloom into bil-lowing paragraphs, whole stories that pivot on that one time you showed up and believed something, or someone, might show up too.

E. B. White said, "A writer who waits for ideal conditions under which to work will die without putting a word on paper."[18] I could say the same for belonging. The conditions are always pretty shoddy when you're getting started.

I already know Margot by way of mutual friends on Facebook. I remember using the word *bananas* as an adjective in my first note to her, and she still "friended" me, which says a lot. Margot is a fellow faith writer in Durham who strikes me as genuine. I determine this based on the fact that she is somewhere north of forty and holds her hair out of her face with baby claw clips.

It's January when I send Margot another Facebook message with the clause that "it's okay if she doesn't remember who I am, but I know who she is and like what I see and want to see what can come of it." I tell Bess of my plans, and she says she wants to come too. This is just the sort of magnetism Margot holds.

Over tea and fruit at Mad Hatters, the three of us share stories about how we've ended up here. Margot tells us how she is raising three kids while living in a community in Durham that brings able-bodied folks and folks with physical challenges together on a few close blocks. There's also an initiative in the neighborhood called Friendship House composed of divinity school students interested in sharing life alongside persons with disabilities. It's a system both of independence and accountability, hospitality and agency, space and uncomfortable closeness.

"Did you always feel it was your vocation to work with people like that?" I ask, leaning closer.

Her eyes light up under her purple-specked glasses.

"Heavens, no," she answers. "I worked with youth for a number of years and was so bad at it; I have such a thin skin. It wasn't until I learned about working with folks who have disabilities that I knew, 'That's the kingdom. And I want in.'" She elaborates, "That's the great thing about the people I get to spend time with now. They don't reject me. There is just this radical, unyielding acceptance."

I want that. I glimpsed it in the short amount of time I had spent in the women's prison. Now I wonder if there are whole pockets of people I have been missing in an effort to find my tribe, the kind of people who wouldn't let me hold them off with elbow straight. The apostle James writes that religion at its purest is to care for orphans and widows in need (James 1:27). I am beginning to suspect my belonging is somehow in their hands.

At the end of our conversation, I say to Margot, "Maybe I'll see you at church sometime," and she says, "Yeah, but I probably won't say hi. I usually make a beeline for the door when worship is over."

Her honesty makes me laugh.

"Me too," I say. "Me too."

It happens unexpectedly.

Scurrying out of the sanctuary after the early morning service, not wanting to talk to anyone and not wanting to gather my things slowly in hopes that someone might talk to me, I am the first to the doorway where Martin stands greeting people as they leave. I wonder what he thinks of these early exiters, but true to my Catholic upbringing, I've hung around long enough for the closing hymn.

As I approach him, I smile and stick out my hand. He takes it. His eyes crinkle. And he says, clear as day, "Good to see you again, Erin."

He knows my name.

It is as if God has spoken over me, Father Mitch and my parents too.

To show up in a place of worship is no guarantee that transformation will happen, that I will live differently as a result, that I will be made well by prayers, that I will find a community that cares. Nor is it to say that because God promises to show up here with me that God will not show up there with you. What I mean when I say that God shows up in a place is that I am able to witness the presence of God, palpably, both because the biblical witness tells me this is where my people have known God to dwell and because the present witness shows me how my people make an invisible God visible. By showing up at church, week after week, my body begs a witness greater than its own two eyes can see. It says, "I cannot do this alone, even though I try."

I walk to the bike rack with cheeks flushed, lifting my eyeglasses up off my nose and wiping the perspiration beneath them. After all of my lessons in showing up, it's time to consider sticking around.

Lesson Four

THE RISK OF VULNERABILITY

Let's face it. We're undone by each other.
And if we're not, we're missing something.

JUDITH BUTLER

Two and a half years. Come winter we have been in Durham two and a half years. You can't get away with skimming the surface of relationships for two and a half years. The first year or two are easier to maintain. Around every bend is a morsel of hope that this church might just nurture, this friendship might just feed, this work might just sustain. It's the thrill of the chase that keeps you going. *You never know,* you say to yourself, *you never know how it might all turn out.*

We had a phrase in college for that moment in a relationship when you ask the question that you can't not ask: "What are we?" It's called the DTR—or the "defining the relationship" talk—and, if you could, you held out as long as possible before looking all out of sorts about it. You wanted the other guy to ask first. You weren't sure you wanted to know the truth. You knew that sometimes not knowing was the more romantic of the two options. But not knowing kills you a little inside.

I've been flirting with Outpost Community Church with no official status for six months, and I want to know now if they'll have me. I want to know if I'll have them, too, and figure out why I'd want them anyway. The only thing I've joined in the last year is the local Costco, and there I only turn up once a month for the essentials, like peanut-butter pretzels and toilet paper. Would being a card-carrying member of a church be much different?

The truth is I haven't always been able to figure out how to take the next step toward belonging. To do so, I am going to have to expose myself in ways that feel needy and, well, gross.

I figure a new members' class should do the trick.

᠎ ᠎ ᠎

The problem, as I see it, with church membership is that it's like signing up for one big group project. You're bound to get stuck working with that guy who likes to "hear himself think" or that gal who "would do it in a heartbeat" if it weren't for her chronic mono or chronic children. In the end, whatever gets eked out, you'd rather not put your name on it.

I've never considered joining a local church before showing up for my first Inquirers' class in February. I joined the Catholic Church when I was twelve, but my commitment never felt tied to a particular people or place. It was more like I was registering to vote: Catholic? Protestant? Independent? The ideology was what was important, and other than an uncomfortable conversation with your father on polling day, mostly people didn't check up on you to see if your public label matched your private choices.

I don't think I've ever looked forward to going to church for the people. The closest I came was when I was attending a nondenominational church with Perk in high school. When my parents divorced, although Perk was still taking Charlie and me to Mass, she wanted us to be able to find our own faith identities as we grew older. Dad disagreed; we were Catholics, and Catholic was what we would stay. Searching for an impartial opinion to their impasse, they put the decision in the hands of a Jewish arbitrator. At ten and eight respectively, Charlie and I were summoned to give an official opinion on the matter. This time the questions came in a dark, lawyerly room overlooking Lake Michigan. Why do you want to explore other churches? We complained about what kids complain about: the chanting, the repetition, the hierarchy. Why go through a priest when Perk told us we had a direct line to God? When the arbitrator's report came back, Perk fell to the floor. Our answers were too close to hers; "brainwashed" was the exact word. We were ordered to continue attending Catholic Mass until we were eighteen and able to form a theology of our own. Mom had no choice but to obey the decision, homeschooling us for part of our catechism classes until we were confirmed into the Catholic Church. By the time I was fourteen, she had started going to an evangelical church on her own, and I, in a strange kind of teen rebellion, followed her against orders.

Hands raised high, emphatic clapping and public prophesy ignited something inside of me. So did the boys. In fact, as much I loved watching Perk dance in the side aisle of the twenty-row chapel with a grin wide across her face, the people I was most eager to see each week were the nominally Christian boys who attended, although I had never had much success with them. I kissed one of them in the second-floor bedroom of a tract home, but he never returned my calls, and I reminded myself he had a shiny forehead. Another I invited to go to prom with me, seeing as how the dating pool at my high school was more like a cesspool, but when I asked him after the dance if he ever thought about being more than friends, he said, "Uh-uh," and I quickly assured him, "Me neither." One of my youth group leaders, a spry twenty-something named Shannon, invited me to go to the young adults fellowship with her, but despite my hunger for deeper discussion, there wasn't much possibility for deeper relationships. No one wanted the liability of hanging out with a sixteen-year-old past ten o'clock on a Friday.

With the mating game off the table, connecting with my fellow Inquirers at Outpost is decidedly less attractive. During the icebreaker, I am puzzled by one woman's description of a favorite dessert called "white trash" and annoyed when a young, athletic-looking man answers, "Does fruit count?" I'm looking for answers to more intimate questions, like, "What in God's name are you doing here?" Still, I write their names in the margins of my binder with care: Masie, Avery, Jessica, Sandra, Jack, Becca, Ralph, Marie, Jenny, Louis, Laurie, Gregg and Martin.

"We don't have a lot in common," Martin begins, "but we're here because of our faith in Jesus Christ." There's a form tucked into the front sleeve of our binder with a space for our name, address and whether we are the "head" or "spouse" of our family. I draw a big, lopsided circle around both. It also asks what kind of membership we're seeking; there are three options: to become a new member by way of baptism, to transfer membership from another church, or to reaffirm your faith if your old church, like the Catholic Church, won't recognize the switch.[1] There's also something called affiliate membership for those who want to keep their membership at their home church, but I think this seems the worst of all the options. Committing to one church is hard enough.

"Are we being graded separately?" I want to ask God after our first class is over, but I have a feeling I won't like the answer.

≡ **25** ≡

"Community cripples," Bess preaches in a sermon, and I nearly open my mouth to shout "Amen!" before remembering that's not the kind of thing young white girls from Michigan take to doing. I notice two men walk out when she takes the pulpit.

When we embrace the community Christ embraced, we are thrown off balance, she says. Recall the story in the book of Genesis when Jacob wrestles an angel of God and leaves the encounter with a limp. Or the lynchpin narrative of the Christian faith in which Christ wrestles our sin and takes on the limp of humanity. Jacob's limp prepares him to accept the embrace of his brother Esau. Christ's limp prepares us to accept the embrace of God. The limp of the church is what prepares us to embrace one another. "Sometimes, though," Bess admits, "this bond feels more like a handicap than a blessing."

Christians often refer to the church as the body of Christ. We quote the apostle Paul, "So we, who are many, are one body in Christ, and individually we are members one of another" (Romans 12:5). John Calvin lifts up the unity of the church, writing, "As they depend upon one head, so they grow up together as into one body."[2] But we often don't talk about how the church is a vulnerable body. It can't not be if the body on whom our life together is patterned is the vulnerable body of Christ.

⊟ ⊟ ⊟

One of my favorite stories in the New Testament is told in the fifth chapter of Mark's Gospel. It's about a hemorrhaging woman who's made many attempts to get well. But much to her embarrassment, her body still bleeds uncontrollably. It's been bleeding for twelve years. And now it's impoverished her financially and emotionally. Mark describes her disease using the Greek word *mastix*, "a graphic expression meaning 'whip, lash, scourge, or torment.'"[3] She's tortured by shame.

Still, after years of suffering, this woman hasn't lost her hunger for healing. If she had, I can't imagine she would have even ventured outside the day Jesus passed by in the crowd. But she doesn't do this. She gets off the couch, leaves her house and finds Jesus in the crowd. And not only does she find him, she has the wild idea to touch him. What's even wilder is that it works. Mark notes, "Immediately her hemorrhage stopped; and she felt in her body that she was healed of her disease" (Mark 5:29).

The story's not over though. At the same moment the woman is healed, Jesus feels in his own body a strange loss of power and asks, "Who touched my clothes?" as if he doesn't know. Maybe he doesn't. Some biblical scholars have tried to explain away his apparent ignorance by proposing that Jesus knew who touched him but wanted to draw out the "culprit" so that she could make a profession of faith.[4] Many of us have heard about this kind of God, the puts-us-to-the-test-so-that-we-can-experience-a-teachable-moment kind of God. God in this approach is like a well-meaning parent who tells a white lie every now and then to make a point but who nevertheless is always in control. The problem with this approach is that it seeks to impose a sort of "reasonable" explanation for Jesus' vulnerability that Mark never reveals. (Gospel writers Matthew and Luke tell it differently.) It makes you wonder, what are we afraid will happen if our God is the vulnerable kind of God?

Vulnerability has long been considered a trait of the weak. The disease of perpetual bleeding that plagued the hemorrhaging woman would have been a particularly devastating affliction in both ancient Greco-Roman and Judaic culture. Not only did it mark the body as feminine in its connection to the reproductive cycle, but it also signified the embarrassing leakiness of vulnerable bodies. Because the dominant medical model of the time believed women were "Gollum-like creatures"[5] whose dampness was regulated only by regular menstrual cycles, the early audience of the gospel would have likely found the hemorrhaging woman's disease doubly repulsive in both its display of feminine irregularity and bodily disability. They might also remember Jewish purity laws cited in Leviticus 15:25-33 that maintained high regard for bodily and social regulation. A woman who bled in excess of her menstrual cycle was deemed unclean and further isolated from her community.

That's what's so remarkable about Mark's Gospel. In it Jesus is presented as a God who is willing to literally trade places with one of society's most vulnerable. Over the course of the healing, the woman's body becomes strong as Jesus' body becomes permeable. Yet Jesus doesn't condemn her for causing this strange outflow of power but blesses her neediness as a sign of faithfulness. He says, "Daughter, your faith has made you well; go in peace, and be healed of your disease" (Mark 5:34). After years of suffering in isolation, the hemorrhaging woman is grafted into the kingdom as a *daughter* of God. For her body to become stable, Jesus becomes porous. For her soul to find salvation, Jesus becomes sin. Philosopher Judith Butler claims it is the vulnerable body that binds humanity together.[6] In the Christian tradition, it is the vulnerable body of Christ that binds the church together.

≡ ≡ ≡

The church is like a bunch of first graders running a race, Bess reasons, in which each of our legs is wrapped with a piece of crepe paper attached to the neighbor beside us. If we are to move toward the finish line without breaking the fragile bond between us, we will have to time our steps in unison, moving slowly and looking silly but headed in the same direction. Sure, each of us could move faster unencumbered. But this race is not about efficiency.

This race is about the reality of our interconnectedness, a reality we often acknowledge in our heads rather than our hearts. Too often we stop asking others to collaborate with us at work or read our essay for feedback or help co-lead a workshop because we can do it better ourselves. It's easier that way. We stop celebrating our personal joys with one another—the launch of a book, the conception of a baby, the landing of a new job—because we don't have the time or energy to fill people in. It's easier that way. We stop telling people about our failing marriage or borderline eating disorder or embarrassing blister because, practically speaking, what do they know about it? It's easier this way.

It's delusional this way too. Albert Einstein called our feelings of separateness "a kind of optical delusion of consciousness" by which we think we can function apart from the embrace of one another.[7] The scientific word for this reality is *entanglement*, and according to principles discovered by quantum physicists, entanglement pervades every inch of nature so that even after separation occurs between two previously related particles they continue to act as one, shifting and changing in response to one another.[8] It is at once terrifying and exhilarating to be so dependent on the actions of another, our bond as tenuous as crepe paper and as enduring as atoms.

A quick note here that not all of us have the privilege of choosing vulnerability; some bodies, like many of my classmates' in the women's prison, are made vulnerable by force. Jesus said of his own body, "No one takes it from me, but I lay it down of my own accord" (John 10:18). Vulnerability is a gift to ourselves and others when it's a choice we make and not a right exploited. God does not ask us to be crippled by community so that a few may dominate the others but so that all may be dependent on each other. That's the marvel of the church. Where other institutions ask us to bring our best self, put on our can-do face and save the world one problem at a time, the church allows us to start from the ground of our true being, a humanity fragile and flawed and dusty from the wrestling. "More than a sociological institution subject to human limitations," theologian Susan Wood writes, "[The church] is the body of Christ and temple of the Spirit."[9] When we risk belonging to one another as we are, limping though we may be, we become a house for the holy.

26

I have been practicing speaking my need lately. It goes something like this. We're sitting around shooting the breeze when I say, "I need more intimate friendships in my life," or "I need intergenerational relationships at church," or even "I need to talk about this later because I don't know where to go from here." Maybe you look at me and feel some sort of pity. Or maybe you feel bullied, like I'm trying to manipulate you into meeting my need in some very specific way. But hopefully you look at me and sort of sigh-smile, saying, "I see your need, and I'm reminded of my own."

Life has been a crazy experiment in neediness since graduation. Despite being almost thirty, I still feel awkward trying to make and sustain adult friendships. It was Rush who suggested vulnerability might be one of my "challenge areas" when I came home from another friend date with someone I found nice enough but with whom there was no spark.

"I don't know. It's not like I felt she was holding anything back. It's just that, well, I don't know how deep we can really go," I explained to him. This felt like an adult-like observation, focused on conserving energy in relationships rather than spreading myself thin.

"How deep are *you* willing to go?" Rush pushed back. This was the problem with telling your husband that you wish he would give you more feedback, that in the scheme of the whole Christian principle to "speak the truth in love," he seems to be too good at the "love" part and skimpy on the "truth."

By speaking my need, I'm trying to be clearer now with people about what I'm after. Hopefully they will say, "That's what I'm after too." But maybe they'll say, "I don't really share your need, but I know someone who does and you should give them a call." The thing with neediness is you're grateful for the morsels.

I tried doing this with a new group of friends I wanted to be intentional with. I sat each of them down and said, "I need community. And I need it to be regular. Not like every Tuesday regular, because that depresses me a little, but one serious hangout a month and another more casual one." And each one, God bless 'em, said, "Yeah, I need that too," and so we formed a small group.

Small group. When I hear myself referring to *my* small group or complaining that I don't *have* a small group, it's as if "small group" is something I possess rather than something to which I belong, something I *should* have, along with "quiet time" and a "personal relationship" with God that implies I'm fulfilling my evangelical checklist. Still, for all its vagueness, a small group of Christians with whom I can risk showing up in the flesh is something that I need, badly. It acts as a sort of reality check against a life lived largely in my head.

⊟ ⊟ ⊟

The first small group Rush and I joined as a married couple met at the church across the parking lot from our parsonage. Every Monday night we'd gather with a group of youngish adults in the sitting room off the narthex to study the Bible and plan holiday parties. Folks who rarely piped up with their thoughts on the apostle Paul's instruction for table fellowship had a cookbook's worth of opinions on whether we should serve marshmallow graveyard cake or candy corn popcorn hands at the upcoming Halloween party. On more serious subjects, silence would often fall like a sheet until someone gave up and asked, "Rush, you've been to seminary. What do you think?"

The two of us went to the Halloween party dressed as Britney Spears and her then beau Kevin Federline. I put in hair extensions purchased from the local pharmacy, and Rush wore a mesh hat. We felt sure then that nobody got it, and nobody got us. After a while the group started to unravel, and Rush and I slipped back into a weekly routine of eating leftover pizza and watching *The Bachelorette.*

We tried small group speed dating at our church in California. Come one, come all, you lonely seekers, fraught and fried by the traditional channels of intimacy! Like a barnyard dance, we were corralled into step, first into geographical groupings and then further into our preferred night of the week to meet. It didn't take long before I looked around the room, worried that other groups were laughing more, but I didn't dare try switch. That would have been un-Christian. Instead I tried to relieve my panic with a show of bleary-eyed enthusiasm. Rush and I agreed to host a small group and, sure, send out reminders, and, okay, organize food. There was nothing either of us could do to stop the commitments from tumbling out of our mouths. They stopped on their own after a year, when our small group agreed to go on a break for the summer and never rekindled the flame. Instead, we invited six friends— Christians and doubters and Reiki healers too—to meet monthly with us for dinner and conversation about the things that mattered most. For a while, the truth of our lives became plain.

For two years, Rush and I didn't join a single thing together in North Carolina. The distance between our faith communities in Chapel Hill and Durham felt wider than the fourteen miles that separated us. We came home with different stories of different people with names we hadn't heard and faces we couldn't picture. On the Sundays that he preached, I'd find a car to go hear him. On Sundays when he was off, we'd ride our bikes to Outpost.

"Is your wife still enjoying school?"

"Oh, no, she's long graduated."

"Say hi to that husband of yours, Russ."

"It's Rush, actually, and I will, thanks."

If we joined one of the small groups together at his church, we'd be looking at another logistical logjam. I asked Bess about small groups at Outpost, but the person who coordinated them had just left. Bess was joining an already established one with Henry, and there was room for one more person; did I want to come? "No, thanks. Rush and I need this one thing between us."

"So what should we do, babe?" Rush asked, rocking on the screened-in porch after work one day. "If we don't want to go to a small group at your church, and we don't want to join a small group at mine, what if we did something on our own again?"

Just thinking about the idea made my shoulders sag. It felt as if we were always the ones initiating, scrounging for friendships like raccoons for bones.

For all the blessings of strangers—the mystery they carry and the surprise they bring—there was something to be said for finding your tribe too. We reasoned that a group of ministry couples would be easy; nobody would have to be in charge or relied on for all the answers. Sundays and Wednesdays would automatically be out. We'd make something other than casseroles. There would be wine too. Honesty and hard conversations. Because where else were we going to find those things amongst the politeness of adult friendships?

 ⊟ ⊟ ⊟

I met Juli, like Bess, at orientation for divinity school. She looked like a TV librarian, her hair in a mini beehive and glasses that flared toward her ears. She was carrying around a bag from the realty company we used, and I was newly preoccupied with looking up houses on Realtor.com, convinced that we had chosen the wrong one and sure that if I could prove it to myself, I'd feel better.

"Did you buy a house too?" I asked, sliding in beside her.

She looked up from her lap with brown eyes set behind protective frames. "We did, yeah. My husband, Corey, just started a PhD program. I think we're going to be here awhile."

It didn't take long for the entire entering class of students to separate themselves into lifestyle enclaves: single and looking, newly married and googly, a few years married and hopeful, married of any length with kids, and adults with adult divorces or adult parents to manage. Soon, a loose group of women in our late twenties and early thirties began threading in and out of each other's lives.

Juli and I ate lunch together on the backside of the library. Sometimes conversation stalled out; she could be quiet and I was an oversharer. I would get hot over some bigoted comment in class, and she would be reasonable about it. She was six years older than me, and I wondered if she thought me immature at times. I had reasoned with Enuma, a forty-something writer in town, "Don't think I'm neurotic because I'm young, like it's some habit I'll grow out of. I'm almost sure I won't. I'm almost sure I'll be like my mother."

Juli and I talked about whether our husbands would get along, playing matchmaker in our conversations about how Corey liked college football as much as me and how Rush was an artist much like Juli. We were both pragmatic Midwestern girls with sensitive Southern boys for husbands. Those things mattered, sure, but when the four of us finally met, it was their availability that drew us in. Corey cried and Juli teared up when they shared about their marriage almost falling apart in those early days, and we said we knew what they meant. We, too, had been nasty and mean and unsure—like the time in the Crate and Barrel parking lot when I thought of the best words to pierce a man and growled "failure," or how I'd start to uncontrollably laugh when Rush got upset, and he'd revert to youngest brother mode. We loved each other deeply, but we were so impossibly human. It was hard to stand ourselves sometimes; it was even harder to share ourselves. Availability—both emotional and literal—is a rare gift in a culture in which we schedule coffee dates three weeks out and then barely scratch the surface of our lives before our time slot is up.

It was easier finding friends when I was single. I was available and needy, and eager to feel chosen. The signs of friendship were easier to read then, too, like when I had to write a name down for my college's rooming lottery or make a dinner reservation before the Sadie Hawkins dance. This created some high-stakes drama—feelings were hurt and people were excluded, but I also knew who felt the same way and who just wasn't that into me. Now I found myself capable of blurting out at random, "Do you like me? And secondly, do you have time for me?"

Professor Rebecca Adams was quoted in a *New York Times* article called "Friends of a Certain Age" explaining that the three conditions for adult friendships are "proximity; repeated, unplanned interactions; and a setting that encourages people to let their guard down and confide in each other."[10] Instead of those hyper-intense, lifelong, bridesmaid-worthy friends, most of us in our late twenties and beyond have what sociologists call "situational friends." There are the "divinity school friends" or the "work friends" or the "can afford to eat out once in awhile" friends. Then there are the "Erin friends" and "Rush colleagues" and the "thank God they like us both" friends. We talked about "fitting each other in" like we were squeezing our rounded lives into a square-shaped hole in someone else's calendar.

Now that I have a live-in partner, I don't call friends every day just to see what they're up to, I don't assume we're doing something on a Friday night without emailing a few days in advance, and I don't give them "first-run versions" of my problems unless Rush is in a staff meeting and Perk has turned her phone off. I'm a little less available and a little less needy than I once was for friends. I assume most people getting married and starting families are too.

By the time we invited Juli and Corey to gather with us as a small group, we had met Taylor and Blair, too, through a mutual college friend. Taylor was an ordained Presbyterian pastor nearby, and Blair was an art teacher at the local high school. They, too, had just bought a house in town and were busy buying art and pruning their yard. Here is our need, we said, to create a space where we can meet and talk about God and talk about marriage and make food with our hands. It was tenuous at first. Corey came on strong like he does, and Rush sat back, and Blair said off-the-wall things we weren't sure what to make of. Juli was kind, and I was overeager, and Taylor was guarded. But after a few meals together, the conversations got easier, and the prayers felt genuine, and Blair grew a beard.

In February, we are singing "Happy Birthday" to Juli over carrot cake when Corey blurts out, "We're pregnant!" I squeal so loud Amelia punches my thighs with her two front paws. "We're only eight weeks along, but we wanted you to know," he adds. "I don't know why people wait to share the news. We want to celebrate with you now. And if something bad happens, we want to grieve with you then." Standing on my toes to embrace Corey, I hold on tight and lock my wrists, hoping we can all withstand the change.

= 27 =

The second thing Rush and I start doing together in Durham is care for widows and orphans. Well, not widows and orphans exactly, but homeless parents—mostly mothers—and their children.

Interfaith Hospitality Network is a ministry of local congregations and volunteers who support families in transition. Each week, the families in the program move to a different church or synagogue where they eat their evening meals and spend their nights. During the day, parents either go to work or look for work, and children go to school or daycare. Outpost doesn't have the facilities to host families overnight, but they provide volunteers once every two months when the Episcopal church downtown opens its doors for the week. A volunteer coordinator at Outpost solicits sign-ups for evening volunteers to transport the families to the Episcopal church, meal volunteers to provide dinners for the families and overnight volunteers to sleep in the church parlor.

The first time Rush and I sign up to be overnighters, we ask Bess and Henry if they want to join us. The four of us show up at the Episcopal church with our sleeping bags around 8:30 p.m. Most of the families have already gone downstairs to the adult education rooms, where their cots are laid out. Geoff, Outpost's volunteer coordinator, is in the parish hall with a deck of Uno cards in front of him. "Want to play?" he asks us.

The five of us play Uno for about twenty minutes or so before we hear the buzz of the elevator. A high school girl with brown skin and hair taut appears. She walks past us, eyeing the table of cards. "Jasmine, join us," Geoff bellows. She smirks and disappears into the kitchen.

"Do you know the IHN rules of Uno?" Geoff asks us as he shuffles the cards on the laminate table. We shake our heads. In his late thirties, Geoff has Shakespearean cadence but boyish mannerisms. "Every time you draw a card, you have to count like Dracula. Von, a-too, tha-ree." It's the silliest thing, but by the time Jasmine returns from the kitchen, we're making such a racket—laughing at how into the game Geoff is getting, laughing at how Henry refuses to count, laughing at each other laughing—that she sits down to see what she's missing.

"Can we deal you in?" Bess asks her, and she agrees.

Rush and I make good overnight volunteers. There isn't always a lot of interaction with the families; some we don't even get to meet until we do wake-up calls at 5:30 a.m. the following morning. But we're still young enough to sleep on the diamond-patterned sofas in the parlor and not wake up stiff the next morning. Plus, we don't have any children at home that would require a sitter, only Amelia, who can handle ten hours without a potty break.

Rush and I talked about having biological children when were dating, and then again when we got engaged. Rush was great with kids; I assumed this meant he'd be great with his own.

"Are you sure you can marry me knowing I may never want them?" I asked.

"What makes you think *I* want them?" he asked back. I told myself then I wasn't strong enough for pregnancy. I told myself our marriage wasn't strong enough either. I think the truth was I was scared to suffer.

To welcome the vulnerable means to welcome suffering. I don't know about you, but I'm inclined to take a pass on suffering if I can avoid it. I can hardly watch other people suffer; I make Rush turn off the television after a sporting event because I get so upset by the sour faces of the losing team. But avoiding suffering doesn't seem to be an option in my tradition. Not if I want the good, brave life Jesus promised. There's no Christ without the cross, they say, and there's no church without the Christ. We'll have to suffer more than fools if we are to care for one another.

The second Sunday of the Inquirers' class finds me nowhere near home. Instead, I am on layover in Atlanta. Moving walkways push me from terminal to terminal, and when there is nowhere to go but up, the blinking blue lights of newsstands appear at the top of escalators. We are all wanderers here, trying to make our way to the destination we've set out for and wondering what suffering we'll endure to get there. One of my colleagues, a man with a mindfulness bell that centers him four times an hour, calls the Atlanta airport the "seventh circle of hell."

Halfway between here and there, I am returning from my second facilitator preparation retreat. This one took me to Carefree, Arizona, where Nonchalant Avenue ambled over Lazy Lane, and Bloody Basin eased into Tranquil Trail. For me, it was a bumpier road from hostility to peace. While waiting for a shuttle outside the Phoenix airport, I got spooked by an attendant who assured me that he'd called a driver, but who some forty minutes later was still mumbling into his walkie-talkie. I couldn't help but imagine the worst. A stolen truck. A fake uniform. A trip to a meat-packing warehouse.

I squeezed my duffle bag between my thighs and pretended to be typing on my phone until I remembered I *could* help it. "I'm Erin. What's your name?" I asked, putting down my phone. It didn't take long to learn that Tyronne was getting married soon, although there wasn't a date, or a ring. She had proposed to him, and while he wasn't quite sure about the etiquette of it all, her kids were happy and so was he.

By the time the shuttle arrived, the roads were terrible. A front rose over the desert as we sped along the highway. A small man with a mustache leaned over me to take a picture with his iPhone, and the businesswoman in front of us said she'd never seen such a sight in all her trips here. Our driver, a skinny Filipino man, was the most ecstatic, taking his hands off the wheel to clap. "I've lived here nineteen years. Nineteen years and I've never seen snow." It was sleet, but we hadn't the heart to tell him. When he let me out at the retreat center, he bent down to make a snowball out of the slush, but it fell apart. I handed him a tip while he wiped his dripping hands on his jacket.

I worried now that requesting a single room had been a bad idea, an antisocial move that would alienate me from my cohort of twenty facilitators in training. Don't be ridiculous, I told myself as I entered the oversized room with two queen beds and a wood paneled bar. Any good writer needed a self-imposed streak of insularity. Plus, the possibility of bunking with a snorer was enough to make me belligerent, which seemed even more antisocial in the grand scheme.

Every time I sat down to put a word on the page though, the fear of failure crept in. The fear of saying too much. The fear of having nothing to say. Kathleen Norris calls it the fear of the blank page, but I think it's the fear of the next page too, and the next one, and the one after that. Some of us have the illusion that if we sit with our thoughts long enough, we'll come to the end of ourselves and be found petty and wanting. It's why I'm often the first to leave parties; like Cinderella's carriage at midnight, I fear turning into a sour pumpkin if given just thirty more minutes of small talk. The anecdote to the fear, says Norris, is humility, the ability to "weed out the lies you've told yourself and get real."[11] But lies are not so easily uprooted. Silence is an expert pruner of both the writer's life and the Christian's too.

I skipped the morning meditation the first full day on retreat, but there was still plenty to be had as we sat in a circle of chairs for the next three and learned what it was to create "safe space for the soul to show up"—our souls and the souls of those we hoped to serve. "The soul is like a wild animal," Parker explained to us during one session. "You can't go banging through the forest and expect to find it." With partners and in the large group, we practiced pausing between each other's voices and discerned with patience when to offer our own. David Whyte's poem "The Winter of Listening" stirred us with these words: "How easily you can belong to everything simply by listening."[12]

I gave thanks to God at the end of each day for the end of words. Mine, and others' too. A different sort of community was forming here, one in which I wasn't known for what I said (or wrote) but for how I listened. Oh, the delight of not having to be persuasive! The burden gone of trying to sound relatable! We listened our way into believing that we weren't alone.

On our last night of the retreat, I hustled back to my room after the evening session to put in another good hour of writing. Mary Ellen, a tall blond in her sixties with sharp blue glasses and a warm

Minnesota accent, ran into me in the hallway. "Are you skipping dinner tonight?" she asked. "Mukta got the chef to put out those blond brownies you like so much."

"Oh, I'm not feeling that hungry." The truth was I was tired of eating water balloons dressed as vegetables. Not even another meal comprised mostly of blondies with butterscotch would do.

"C'mon. Can I at least get you a little snack?" I followed her into her room as she disappeared behind the wet bar and started pulling open containers onto the counter. By the time she was through, I had a tub of hummus and pretzels in one hand and a corked bottle of white wine tucked under my armpit. "Left over from last night," she winked. "You missed us drinking out of Brian's boot."

"I heard. I promise I'll come out of hiding later," I said, before ducking out of the doorway.

The wine was warm when I poured it into a plastic hotel cup and opened my laptop to start writing.

It tasted sweet.

⊟ ⊟ ⊟

I return home from Arizona, safely making it through the seventh circle of hell and back to Durham. The next Sunday I meet Martin for a brief make-up session before our third class. There are five classes in all, but, despite Outpost's thoughtful curriculum, this seems hardly enough time to make the decision of membership.

Rush reasoned, "Our new members' class only meets once."

"Once?" I cried and fell into the dining room chair. "Am I the only one who thinks we're all moving a little too fast here?"

I arrive at Outpost in the late afternoon, my canvas bag empty save for a wallet and the blue binder of course materials we were given at the first meeting. The door to the church is locked. There's a buzzer nearby to announce my presence, and after a firm press, the lock unhinges. I look around for the mysterious stranger who let me in but can't be sure who decided I was worthy. As my boots tread past the atrium down the hallway to Martin's office, they hardly make a sound. The reverb is absorbed into some carpeted underworld.

"How are you today, Erin?" Martin asks when I come in.

I can hear it in my voice when I answer him, "Fine, thank you. I appreciate you asking." It's the same voice I used growing up when someone called the home line and I picked up with all the pomp and professionalism of a receptionist, "Hello, this is the Lane Residence, how may I help you?" "Business-time Erin" showed up for all sorts of occasions over the years—during class introductions when I wanted to sound appropriately staid; on interviews where I needed to suppress the lurking squeak of the Midwest; and, worst of all, in conversations with friends or family in which I found my temperature rising as my voice lowered. I could feel "Business-time Erin" starting to descend like the Hulk, but instead of becoming terrifyingly irate, I became terrifyingly rational. Unaffected. Unemotional. Inhuman.

I wonder if Martin is tired of all the faces he's seen put on in this room. Maybe like the hemorrhaging woman approaching Jesus they had come to touch something of the righteous life. Surely a divinity school student or two had come by wanting him to prove this or that theology or to persuade him of this or that theory. Maybe, like Jesus, he needed to be alone after all the wanting left.

Perk used to make a stink about pastors. If they shook her hand and looked askance, she'd bristle. If she made a suggestion and they said give it time, she'd boil. If they only called and never visited after surgery or death or divorce, she declared she was through. Most of us have a tendency toward the same, to make our leaders out to be messiahs instead of messengers. Rush was coming home with rumblings about his own senior pastor and accusations that the man had overstepped boundaries with female subordinates. That's what happens when we treat leaders like saviors, I reckoned. I don't want to commit the same violence against Martin.

He tells me we are waiting for another Inquirer to show up who also missed last week. In the meantime, there are a few questions here and there about what brought me to Outpost—no, I'm not a student, yes, I'm married. When I reveal I'm a Catholic, he laughs and says, "There are many of your kind here."

After a few minutes, the young man with the fiancée lumbers into the room with a hello. Louis is a Pentecostal, I learn, but his soon-to-be wife worships here and so will he. He pulls down his sweater vest and takes a seat in the chair across from me.

We start by finishing the exercise we began our first day of class, a three-columned worksheet that lists biblical references and then two blanks following them for "Human Condition" and "God's Action in Christ." It goes something like this: In Romans 6:15-22, we are portrayed as slaves to sin, but now in Christ we are slaves to obedience. In 2 Corinthians 4:3-6, we are blinded by sin, but now in Christ we are a light in the darkness. I put a check mark in my binder next to the reference in Ephesians 2:12-22. While Gentiles like me were once strangers to God's covenant with the Jews, now in Christ we are citizens of one broke-down body that broke through divisions between us.

Later that evening in class, we talk about what it means to be a member of this broken body, more specifically the Presbyterian body, and I am more and more anxious that whatever it is I am being asked to do, I cannot do it. This being our third official meeting, there's only one class left to decide before our final gathering, and I am feeling stuck somewhere between column B and column C, somewhere between here and home.

I learned about my parents' divorce on the same four-post bed where I learned about Jesus. Nobody really remembers it. When I call each of my parents to see what details have lingered, they both say the same thing, "The only thing I'm sure of is that we told you it wasn't your fault." I ask Dad how we reacted to the news, and he says, "You seemed okay with it." We probably were on the surface.

Soon after the split, I developed the peculiar habit of sleepwalking. It was always the same shtick. I was away from home, usually in some hotel room or at some sleepover, when I'd get up from bed in the middle of the night and walk to the door. If it was latched, I unfastened the locking mechanism before letting myself out. The noise often awakened some half-alert adult nearby who asked, "Where are you going, Erin?" It didn't matter if I let myself out the front door of the Holiday Inn or the attic bedroom of my grandmother's neighbor, the answer never wavered. "I'm going home," I'd say. Once, at a friend's house, I stumbled into her parents' bedroom in the night and started filling their suitcases with clothes. Going home, apparently, required a wardrobe change.

Homesickness turned into full-blown anxiety attacks when I had to part with one of my parents at the airport to fly the hundred-some miles between Chicago and Detroit. Perk gave me an angel pin the size of my pinkie pad to wear when we were apart. I'd squeeze it, my lower lip trembling, as the flight attendant showed Charlie and me to our seats. One time a young steward offered me a pair of plastic wings to stop crying. My stomach shook so badly, I leaned forward over my safety belt and the wings fell to the floor.

Charlie jabbed me in the ribs, "Hey, I bet if you keep that up, he'll put us in first class."

I looked up at him, grateful for the distraction. "You think?" I wailed louder and Charlie turned on the charm when the young man came back to our row.

"Would it make you feel better if you could be near me at the front of the plane?"

I shook my head yes and asked, "Can my brother come too?" Charlie looked up at the man with a face as angelic as the cherub on my chest.

"Uh, sure. Your brother can come too."

When we were safely out of view, Charlie gave me a high five and said, "Nice work, E."

Even before my parents divorced, Charlie and I were each other's sanity. When I was three years old, doctors discovered my hearing was faulty and put tubes in my ears. Unacquainted with the filtered sound of my voice, I became incomprehensible to the rest of the family, except for Charlie, who convinced everyone—me included—that he knew what my murmurings meant. "She wants a grilled cheese," he'd report, or, "She wants to help pick up my toys."

A few years after my tubes came out, Charlie awoke stunted in his own speech. Sputtered words and phrases escaped, but sentences were trying. His eyes twitched and his body shook as he struggled to form vowels. No longer able to say my name with ease, he began to call me "Miss E" or Missy, the first of many nicknames he doled out in our family. He had so many words wandering through his head; he couldn't get them out fast enough. Like a blood clot, they hardened in his body, blocking life-giving passages. As we grew older, when strangers called for him, he'd drop the cordless phone on my lap and ask me to talk. He relied on me for all sorts of tasks, like asking a sales associate where the restroom was or ordering a new fleece from the Sears catalog. When we began flying every other weekend between Mom and Dad, we were each other's constants, the only sure home that would be there on either end of the journey.

I stuck near to Charlie through high school, idolizing him and protecting him all the same. When Charlie and his friends needed a fourth to play basketball in the driveway, I put on my snuggest jellies and went man-to-man on the short one. When he bought a 1986 Toyota Camry with the money he'd saved from Showtime Cinemas, I begged him to teach me how to drive a stick shift. But when he left Michigan for the West to become a ski bum, study viticulture and make coffee for a living, I finished high school, moved to the South and got married at twenty-two.

After our fourth meeting of the Inquirers, I ask Martin if we can meet privately. I am getting cold feet about making my home here.

"How did *you* come to belong at Outpost?" I ask Martin, sitting in his office for the second time. He starts to answer, and I realize he's not sure what I mean. Or why I am asking about something different than "When did you come to know Christ?" or "How long have you been a pastor?" But to be fair, it's not his question. Maybe it's not even his generation's question. It's mine.

I have more questions for him, questions about confession and why we focus so much on our own sin instead of God's grace. I ask about Communion and why we don't do it more often here. The sacraments seem to be one of the few ways the church is different than any other volunteer organization, civic group or all-around do-gooder society. Confession and Communion are both sacraments in the Catholic Church. So, too, is confirmation, the ritual of becoming a mature member in Christ's body.

I was confirmed in the seventh grade. While I envied my Jewish friends and their elaborate Bat Mitzvahs, I still reveled in being treated like one of the adults. For one, I got to choose my own spiritual mentor—the obvious choice being Aunt Trish, also known as "Trish the Dish" or the aunt who wasn't afraid to make frank conversation with a twelve-year-old—and two, I got to rename myself. I chose the name Esther to remember the young Jewish queen in exile who had to decide if she would try to fit in or risk being put out. In the end, it's her striking ability to do both that saves her and her people.

"I've thought about it, and I just don't know if I am ready to join yet," I tell Martin while picking my cuticle.

Martin shifts his weight in the chair across from me. "And that's fine, Erin. People make their decisions at their own pace."

"Well, the thing is, if I'm being honest, I just don't know what the point is. I mean, really, what changes if I join the church that I couldn't get by just showing up here and getting involved on my own?" I press.

The popularity of a new-member class is relatively recent in American Protestantism. According to one study, the number of churches requiring such classes doubled from 1997 to 2005.[13] Thom Rainer, who conducted the 1997 study, did an informal poll in 2013 via Twitter and found the number of churches requiring a class had gone from around 17% in 1997 to as much as 86% of those polled in 2013.[14] It used to be that church membership was synonymous with birth. In medieval Europe, only Jews and Turks were considered to be outside the bounds of church participation.[15] During the Reformation, questions of church membership had more to do with who was in the "true church" or the "invisible church" than who was on the attendance rolls. The role of the local church body was more to hold its congregants accountable to moral conduct and governance than it was to address any modern notions of community building.[16] At Outpost, a member is considered a full, participating "citizen" of the church who can vote at budget meetings and serve as elder, neither of which seems all that appealing.

Maybe it was because church offices were never held out as options for me when I joined the Catholic Church that they hold little resonance for me now. At our confirmation, the bishop stretched his arms out over the crowd of preteens and beckoned the Holy Spirit, "Fill them with the spirit of wonder and awe in your presence." Through this proverbial laying on of hands, we remembered the Spirit of God poured out at Pentecost. So, too, did we remember our baptism, a belonging once chosen for us but now a responsibility we accepted for ourselves. Historically, baptism, confirmation and First Communion took place at the same time, one right after the other. I think there's wisdom, though, to the modern sequence of events. We belong to God from birth, and yet it takes years before we are able to respond with a commitment of our own.

Becoming a member at Outpost reads like a marriage ceremony. We are asked to sign a white sheet of computer paper titled "My Covenant with God and the Outpost Congregation." In quotes, it reads, "I accept this congregation as God's family and my family." There are vows, too, that Outpost requires. Public ones. Ones about "active participation" and "faithful attendance." It's not these that scare me. I, like many of my peers, am hungry for clearer and higher standards of belonging. No, there's something about all those "I dos" we'd be saying that reminds me of my wedding day. And it reminds me who would be missing from the ceremony.

My Aunt Julie gave me a rosary on the day of my confirmation. In the note that accompanied it, I learned it belonged to my great-grandmother Gladys. Gladys had been a Catholic woman before she met Grannie Annie's father, a demanding widower named Miles Myers. It wasn't just her faith that he asked her to give up when they married but the hope of having any children of her own. Miles explained that little six-year-old Annie couldn't bear to have siblings. Gladys would be responsible for ensuring that never happened. Despite agreeing to these terms, Aunt Julie reflected, "She must have drawn the line somewhere because her commitment to Catholicism was a never-ending source of irritation for him. She was a quiet believer, and it wasn't until after his death that she began practicing again." Once a Catholic, always a Catholic, or so the saying goes. My family of origin will not let me go.

Nothing about joining this church feels right the more I sit with it. Did it matter that I was already confirmed into the church? Did it matter that I was already covenanted to my husband as one flesh and not to be torn asunder by the distance of two churches? Or was I just overreacting about the whole entire thing, a case of twenty-something commitment phobia?

My mother got cold feet on her wedding day. Her mother told her it was only nerves.

Lesson Five

THE EDGE OF DISCERNMENT

*My humanity is caught up,
is inextricably bound up, in yours.
We belong in a bundle of life.*

DESMOND TUTU

31

There are plenty of bad excuses for not joining a church. "I'm not getting fed" or "I don't like the worship music" or "I just haven't gotten around to it" come to mind. I can't toss any of those well-worn stones at this place. Even the common complaint "I don't agree with everything the pastor says" falls flat as I've gotten to know the man. After almost a year of dating, the most honest reason I could give for leaving Outpost at the altar was, "I feel lost here." What of that excuse?

When I tell Martin of my decision not to join the church in March, he says, "I applaud you for taking this seriously. I wish you could convince other young people to do the same. The most radical thing I ever did with my life was confess Jesus as Lord."

I nod. "I'm not all that interested in convincing them. What'll convince them most is your joy. Tell them about that."

There hasn't been a lot of joy going around these days. It's the season of Lent in the Christian liturgical year, a time of self-denial that begins on Ash Wednesday with these words, "Remember, you are dust and to dust you will return." As much as I take comfort in knowing I'm just a speck in the eye of the universe, I worry about how self-denial gets internalized by those who have already been made to feel small. Instead of being a place where we gather to feast on the gift of one another's presence, the church has been a place where some individuals' gifts are diminished or downright rejected.

I've always thought that in healthy community one becomes more themselves, not less—more aware of their gifts, not less; more true to the image of God, not less. In Galatians 5:14, the apostle Paul reminds mature believers that all instruction for Christian community can be summed up in Jesus' command to "love your neighbor as yourself." But to love our neighbor, we first need a sense of self—and one strong enough to consider loveable. Perhaps it's why Paul warns the believers in the next verse, "Be careful that you don't get eaten up by each other!" (CEB). Community should refine us, not consume us. If I feel less than myself at Outpost, as I did for a time in marriage, who exactly is to blame?

≡ ≡ ≡

"Jasmine pearl, please. For here." I feel for change in the zipper pocket of my wallet while scanning the café. I don't know who exactly I'm looking for. Marcia and I have emailed a few times before arranging to meet, but no picture popped up next to her email address that would clue me in to her appearance. I, on the other hand, am unsure how to describe myself these days other than to say average height, short hair, brown with blonde highlights, or was it blonde with brown lowlights now?

Marcia heads up a nonprofit called the Religious Coalition for a Nonviolent Durham. For those outside its reach, the city of Durham has a gritty reputation: a tobacco town that went bust after the boom. Just fifteen years ago, the city center was barren, with empty storefront windows and outdated buildings the color of dirt under fingernails. While much of the city has experienced an urban revival, spurred largely by the influx of the creative class, it still wrestles the stigma of being dangerous. Fine by us, we say, those who benefit from its trendy restaurants, microbreweries and hipster-friendly shops. "Keep Durham Dirty" bumper stickers hug the back of beat-up Toyota sedans and brand-new hybrids alike. Our scrappiness is a source of pride. But for many of our neighbors, danger is a real threat. Scrappiness is a mode of survival. Although our crime rate is lower than that of more distinguished cities throughout the state, someone is murdered in Durham, on average, every two weeks.[1] Many more grit their teeth in grief.

For almost two decades, Marcia has been calling families who've lost loved ones in violent deaths. She often reads about a shooting or stabbing in the newspaper, the victims of which are disproportionally black men. These murders do not make front-page news. Front-page news goes to the deaths of white girls. Next she searches for the names and telephone numbers of those closest to the deceased. There's no proselytizing after she introduces herself, only a simple question, "Would you like to tell me about your loved one?" Then she listens. To the details. Mostly details about how he always rinsed his dish after a meal or liked to write poetry on the porch.

After they are through remembering aloud, Marcia says, "We want to honor your beloved with our presence at a prayer vigil." They almost always say yes. These vigils rarely take place in a church building; instead, they are often led by local religious leaders near the scene of death. On sidewalks and street corners and front stoops, the vigil is a visible sign to the neighborhood that light overcomes darkness. It's also a sign that what happens at the edges of Durham's economy matters, and not just to the people most affected by it, but even to those largely protected from it.

When I turn around with my oversized cup of tea, my eyes meet with a woman in her fifties with wavy hair and big eyes. She looks at me for a second before we both soften and step toward each other. "Marcia?" I ask, sticking out my hand. She stretches her arms out for a hug. I laugh, embarrassed by my formality, and give in.

I'm here on official business today. Part of my work with the Center for Courage & Renewal is learning about how other like-minded folks and organizations create spaces for real connection, trustworthy leadership, authentic relationships, that sort of thing. Marcia cowrote a book called *Living Without Enemies: Being Present in the Midst of Violence*, in which she advocates for relationships that hinge on *being with* rather than *working for* the needy among us. It sounds impossibly earnest, annoyingly simple, as if it has little to do with me and doing good.

Stillness is the purpose of the prayer vigil ministry. Marcia describes it this way:

Every vigil is different, but they usually last thirty minutes; periods of silence within them might last a minute at a time. Staying still requires embodying and expressing many paradoxes. It means living in the knowledge that everything we need, everything, all the goodness, is here, now. You can only really get that when you're still. When you're busy, when you're going from point A to point B, when you have an agenda, the faster you go and the more judgmental you become, the more determined you are that your perception of reality will prevail.[2]

In the stillness of community, reality reveals itself to us. What does this mean? Stillness not only brings the absence of activity but also the awareness of the reality around us. So too does stillness offer the rare gift of quietude needed to discern the reality within us. How is it with our souls? What lies do we need to weed? What truths do we need to plant?

Parker Palmer describes the paradox of spaces like the prayer vigil as the experience of "being alone together." To rightly understand *who* we are and *whose* we are, he writes, "We need both the interior intimacy that comes with solitude and the otherness that comes with community."[3] One without the other wields a certain kind of violence. With too much solitude, we risk indulging our ego; our version of events becomes *the* version of events. With too much community, we lose touch with our intuition and the voice of God that speaks to each of us, if not in words, then in images, dreams and gut instincts.

Before business meetings—even casual friend dates—I often get a tickle in my stomach. What if this person gets me? What if it's easy just this once? What if this is the moment I look back on and say, "It started then, when we met in the crowded café and talked too loudly for the undergraduates studying nearby." When I sip the last dregs of tea, Marcia seems to be this person, so very much this person that I want to claim her as my Durham mom like some younger version of those adopt-a-grandparent programs we signed up for in elementary school.

We spend more than an hour exchanging ideas for collaboration; maybe she'll come to one of our retreats, or maybe I'll facilitate one of her grief support circles. After we bus our dishes, I shift my computer bag from my right shoulder to the left, less out of necessity than of my nervousness over goodbyes. Go in for a hug, I coach myself, but before I can lean forward, Marcia braces her arm on mine and says abruptly, "You're a feminist, right?"

I can't remember if it came up earlier in our conversation or if I let slip an Alice Walker reference, but I say, a bit slow, "Uh, yeah."

Her eyes get bigger. "Tell me then. I've been away from church for some time now. Where should I go?"

There isn't time to explain. Yes, I go to a church. No, I decided not to join it. Yes, I am a feminist. But no, I don't think you'd like it there. Yes, I like it there. But, the people you love, the people you practice *being with* at prayer vigils, those people are largely not there.

Unlike most churches, the prayer vigil is a space without much of an agenda. You could stand next to a pregnant pastor or a balding drug dealer and it didn't really matter, because you weren't there to convince one another of anything. You were there to bear witness. To grief and the joy that persists. To God and the people that subsist.

I can't offer Marcia much better than that.

= 32 =

When I first showed up at Outpost last May, Amendment One had been newly passed in the North Carolina legislature. For weeks leading up to the vote, Rush and I could walk around our neighborhood and lose track of the number of signs that read, "Another Family Against the Amendment." In one yard, blue wooden posts with painted red letters said, "Our neighbors, coworkers, family, parishioners, friends and their children are not second-class citizens." In another, a sign admonished us to "Love thy neighbors."

Amendment One clarified the state constitution's definition of marriage as a union between a man and a woman only, thus effectively banning the legal recognition of same-sex marriages. Many who had been against the amendment throughout the state blamed North Carolina's more rural communities for its passage. Others chalked it up to a generational gap, citing that older voters were both more civically active and more likely to oppose legislation that diverged from traditional values. In Durham, the result of the vote was nearly flipped in comparison to statewide results, with 70 percent of voters casting their ballots against the ban on same-sex marriages.

Although the Presbyterian Church (USA) of which Outpost is a part is considered a "mainline" Protestant denomination, often aligned with a commitment to social justice and ecumenicalism, it has within its folds strands of evangelicalism. Outpost began as a Presbyterian mission to Durham's millworkers. What remained a blue-collar community for the early part of the twentieth century shifted in the 1960s to becoming a hub of intellectualism due to the closing of the nearby textile mill and the influence of the nearby university. Despite its changing demographics, Outpost remained committed to being a place of welcome during the civil-rights era and was among the first mainline churches to integrate whites and people of color. I can't say for sure where the majority of congregants at Outpost fall on the political spectrum now, and I figure this is just as well.

Before I moved to the South for college, there were only two kinds of Christians in my imagination: Catholics and everybody else. Even after a graduate degree in theology, I still feel like I'm playing catch-up learning the ins and outs of denominationalism. During the Inquirers' class, I learned that Outpost is part of a subgroup within the denomination called The Fellowship of Presbyterians. The Fellowship formed in response to a 2011 decision within the denomination to allow for the ordination of openly gay clergy. While local presbyteries or governing bodies would still exercise discernment over which individual leaders to hire, pressure to conform to the new standard of inclusivity (whether by coercion or threat of dismissal) left some feeling at odds with their consciences. Many pastors and laity chose to leave the denomination altogether. Those who joined the Fellowship opted to remain but with renewed vigor for the values they held essential and a network of like-minded churches to hold them accountable. One of the chief concerns of the Fellowship is the "chronic infighting" on politically divisive issues within the denomination that, in their words, distract from the important work of "making disciples of Jesus Christ."[4] In this way they see themselves as missionaries, called to spread the gospel message to a troubled denomination. Through this evangelistic lens, Martin, an early joiner to the Fellowship, described the mission of our congregation.

I seem to be doing this kind of thing all the time. Plopping myself down in congregations a bit more conservative than I, even—I'll admit—a bit more evangelical than I'm comfortable with. Once, when a reader described my viewpoint as "progressive evangelical," I asked Rush, "Can you believe it? They think I'm an evangelical!"

He cocked his head and laughed. "Erin, that's not surprising."

"Is it true though?"

He thought for a moment. "Well, I don't know. You love Jesus."

"And I love the Bible," I interrupted, "But I don't think it's the only way we can know God."

He pulled me in close, my mouth muted against his chest. "Does it matter?"

It's hard to know what the labels mean: *evangelical, emergent, conservative, liberal, progressive, mainline, missional*; they seem so contextual, geographical, even nonsensical at times. Like a vague job description, these words reveal little until you arrive for your first day of work all suited up. You don't often know what you're getting into until after you've signed on the dotted line. Being married to a pastor, I had withstood more than a few of Rush's job interviews and was left scratching my head at the politics of it all.

⊟ ⊟ ⊟

I remember one particularly unnerving interview Rush underwent. We had been married two years when—right on schedule—I began scrolling through rental listings on Craigslist with the itch to move elsewhere, anywhere. The highlight of my social calendar in the small college town where we lived was Scrabble night with a rambunctious group of older writers and professors.

"How about Chicago?" I asked Rush. Chicago was as good a place as any for me to begin pursuing a career in writing, I reasoned. There was history there too. I liked the idea of returning to the place where I grew up, riding my bike to the marina and putting pennies on the Metra track. I thought it could be like that again.

Rush applied for a job at a nondenominational megachurch, and I submitted an application for journalism school. I got in, despite having named Jerry Falwell as the person I'd most like to interview, and the church hiring committee seemed as much in love with Rush as I was at the time. The whole interview process was rather *involved*, in my opinion. First, they flew him up to Chicago and stuffed him full of questions and deep-dish pizza. Next, a small leadership team flew down to North Carolina, eager to see him in action. Then, they met me.

Sitting around our living room with red wine glasses the size of over-sized Christmas ornaments, Rush answered a steady stream of questions from the leadership team about things like his theology and whether he knew his way around a guitar. When they got to the point of where we'd live if we moved to Chicago, Rush said confidently, "We'll live in Evanston where Erin plans to attend school."

The older man with the bald spot sat up straight on our slip-covered sofa. The furniture in our parsonage had mostly been donated by college friends who had left town and didn't have any more room in their cars full of boxes. The one exception was the loveseat. It had come from a local community clinic where I interned the summer before my senior year. "You don't even want to know how many people have slept on that thing," my coworker Daisy had warned me. I shooed her away and loaded it into the back of Rush's SUV. It occurred to me now that the cushions looked juvenile, unsure of their weight.

"I'll tell you what, Rush," the old one began. "Evanston is a fine place, but we prefer our pastors to live within a five-mile radius of the church."

I cracked a smile before realizing I was the only one who thought this quaint. The tannins from the wine gathered in my mouth, tickling their way down my throat.

"We feel this helps you have an integrated life in the community so you can, uh, bump into youth at the grocery store, attend a soccer game nearby, that sort of thing."

Rush nodded, but stayed firm. "I would definitely consider it after Erin graduates. It's just a yearlong program, and we were hoping that she could be integrated in *her* community while she's a student."

I didn't know where to look. The blond woman wasn't looking at me. Neither was the tall, handsome guy named Ray. They were all leaning forward with jaws tight and eyes tired from travel.

The old one struck again. "Of course, we understand you'd want to support her *career*. But we see your position as a *calling*."

We knew after that. They knew too. It was pointless to even argue with them about their position on women in leadership—they were for it, of course, but unsure that the parishioners could "handle" too much too soon. I asked them if they ever worried whether their parishioners could handle the gospel.

Ray called Rush a few days later to let him know that he was no longer a candidate. "It sounds like you're putting your wife's career above your own," Ray told him.

Rush said, "I'm sorry if it just *sounds* that way."

In the days after, I wanted to cry, but the tears wouldn't come—not even the angry tears I was usually so good at forcing out. I wrote in my journal, "God, where are you calling us? I want to be someplace where we can really be ourselves and use the gifts you've given us. But I also want to be someplace that needs us, uniquely as we are."

It's a hazard of my love affair with tension that I often find myself in communities where my gifts are called into question. But it's that latter desire—the one to feel needed—that often eludes me in churches labeled "liberal." In these churches, it's not so radical for a husband to put his wife first or a woman to preach from the pulpit or a same-sex couple to be wed. Sometimes I imagine these places to be filled with a handful of other Erins, tiny young women full of feminist ideals. They might even have a husband with a beard, too, or a dog named after a fiery redhead from a children's book. It's too easy in communities like these for me not to do the work I am given, because so many other fine souls appear to be stepping up in my stead. How can I find a community in which I feel as if my gifts are *needed* while still feeling like I am *valued*? Put another way, how can I find a church in which there is still work to do in recognizing the full humanity of men and women without feeling like *my* full humanity is lessened by being there?

My friend Andrew says we're not going to get anywhere on politically divisive issues within the church, like gay ordination or women in leadership, until we each name our stake in it. It is not enough to *work for* our brothers and sisters in Christ; instead, we are called to *come alongside* one another, like neighbors at a prayer vigil, and say, "Your diminishment diminishes us all," and likewise, "Your gifts make everyone better."

The megachurch in Chicago seemed like it wouldn't be able to receive the gifts I was bringing as a writer and a wife. Those same gifts found room to breathe when we moved a few months later to Oakland and Rush got a job working in a Presbyterian church. There, too, we found ourselves part of a community divided on the ordination of gay and lesbian pastors. Now here I was again at a church Martin referred to as "an outpost of the kingdom of God," like we were outliers living on the edge of the world. It appeared I rather preferred being an outlier. But even the outlier needs a line to command central.

⊟ ⊟ ⊟

Her name is Georgia. At the end of every service, she climbs the stairs and walks across the wooden platform to the pulpit. Her femininity is refreshing: a thick-heeled pump, a long skirt, and a crow-colored bob accompany her as she receives prayer requests and shared announcements. But my favorite thing about her is the childlike mumble that comes out when she tells us about the opportunity to "Pass the Peas" at the community center next week or invites us to pray for our ministry partners in Thailand. One of the first Sundays I was there, I flipped to the backside of the bulletin to see if she was a pastor. There was just a dash next to her name that read "Caring Ministries." Not long after I started showing up, she announced something about a group of folks interested in civil conversations around the recent vote on Amendment One. I was curious about these bridge builders among us, and so I sent her an email and soon after accepted her invitation to meet them over lunch.

Lunch at Georgia's was a fine time. She and her husband lived about ten minutes from Outpost on a nice plot of land. The house was big but not too big. Perk taught me never to trust an ostentatious Christian. Out of the group of churchgoers gathered, I was the youngest—unless you counted a well-behaved third grader who accompanied her grandmother. I sat with legs crossed in the living room until it was my turn to talk. When I said I led retreats for a Quaker-based organization, some folks seemed truly delighted, Georgia especially. She tells me I'm a "breath of fresh air."

I think she is too.

≡ 33 ≡

The Sunday they confirm my old comrades in the Inquirers' class as new members, I duck out of worship early. I am happy for them, really, but I can't sit still as an onlooker. I'm meeting a friend at the nearby grocery store and don't want to be late. *Besides,* I huff to myself, *it's insensitive that the service regularly goes long. Some of us have a life outside of these walls.*

The cool spring air dances around my neck as I push through the double doors leading out of the sanctuary and trot down the steps. I am pulling at the zipper on my puffy vest when I see him next to the bike rack. I have no choice but to notice him.

He tells his story quickly but purposefully as we stand outside the church—me with my bike helmet hanging off my arm and him with nothing in his hands. He is tall and broad, and he is tired—tired of waking up at 3:00 a.m. from the pokes of police officers telling him to sleep somewhere else, tired of trying to find jobs only to lose them because he can't show up on time, tired of being stared at when he walks into local businesses. He says being HIV-positive makes him tired, too, but he can't afford the medicine.

I know that I am not called to be a single pilgrim in my community, that I am not obligated to solve the problem of homelessness alone, that I cannot privatize this man's pain simply by offering him a place to sleep in my guest bedroom. I know that there are institutions, albeit broken ones, set up to meet such needs. I know that many people without enough food or shelter or clothing choose not to avail themselves of these services. But I am not particularly worried about being duped by these pleas. I am only worried that I will say or do something trite, my cowardliness posing as impatience.

"I don't like to ask for help, ma'am," he stammers, and I cut him off. "It's Erin."

"Erin. I'm Aaron. Isn't that funny?"

"Pretty funny," I muse.

He cocks his hip and continues, "You see I don't like to ask for help, but I'm hungry; I slept outside last night. I need some food."

I pause, wondering what my body will do next. In the interim, "I'm sorry. That sucks."

"It does suck," he nods. "I came here to live with my daddy. Took the bus from Texas and showed up at his door. He took one look at me and decided he didn't want *this*." "This" is a full body gesture that moves from the top of his black head down to his black sneakers, skimming past a pink tank top and cut off shorts. "And he's a pastor. That's messed up, right?"

"Yeah. That's messed up."

He persists. "So can you get me something to eat?"

I look at the bagel shop across the street and reason it won't take more than a few minutes to step in line. "Uh, okay, yeah. How about a breakfast sandwich?"

"I want something hot," he says, "How about the buffet at the grocery store?"

"Okay, the grocery store it is."

We walk side by side to the health food market around the corner, and he towers over me, his body muscular and soft. I ask him if he knows anyone here besides his dad, and he shakes his head. What about back in Texas? There's a mom there who will have him, he says, but he can't scrounge the bus fare to go back. I ask him if he wants to go back, and he changes the subject.

Nobody stares when we get in line at the buffet. Maybe it's because everyone is absorbed in their Sunday rituals of morning papers that follow morning jogs. Or maybe it's because the grocery store is one of those magical places where the need to eat is palpable, whether from a patchouli-cloaked Rastafarian, a bjorn-wrapped baby mama or a cross-dressing homeless man.

When we go to pay, I see the person I am supposed to meet sitting with a paper spread across her table. I hand my credit card over in exchange for his plate full of biscuits.

"I really need to be going now. But really, blessings." I nod. I smile. I wait for him to leave.

"Well, if I could ask one more thing of you. It won't take long," he begins. We are blocking the entrance now. "The thing is, I don't want to sleep out on the streets again. If you give me twenty dollars or so, I could afford to pay for a hotel room tonight. I've used up all the time I got at the shelter for the month."

I shake my head. "I'm not going to give you money. But I tell you what. I go to that church across the street. You know, the one where we met outside. And every Wednesday during Lent we serve supper at 5:30. If you want to come sometime, just wait for me out front and we can walk in together."

"Okay," he says, but his eyes are looking elsewhere now. I doubt he'll take me up on the offer. And if he does, I wonder if he'll feel any more at home there than he does on the streets. Even I feel out of place sometimes when I show up with bedhead and the Michigan T-shirt I've slept in the night before.

He reaches out for a hug, and I don't hesitate this time. He smells like baby powder.

"Hey, Aaron?" I say, as he pushes the door open. "You should go home to your family."

He smiles. "I'll try."

34

Charlie said he had dance parties in Seattle. He would put on records, serious records like Carly Simon or Whitney Houston, and friends would scuff up his wood floors with their man boots and lady oxfords. Charlie said they had progressive dinners in Seattle. Everyone would get on a bike—because everyone had a bike—and they would ride around the city stopping at a different home for every course. Charlie said they made homemade candles and ice cream sandwiches in Seattle. Charlie said he was happy. I hoped I would be happy there too.

It wasn't that I didn't like Durham. Once the chill choked out the mosquitoes our first fall there, I felt at ease again in my California uniform of sweaters and boots. But by the time the cold air was spindling through the floorboards of our new house, I had already found a summer job with the Center for Courage & Renewal on Bainbridge Island, a short ferry commute from the city of sharp peaks and steep streets. I first learned of the organization while working as a book publicist in San Francisco; supporting people in discerning a healthy sense of self and purpose seemed work I was born to do. I dialed the executive director and explained, "These are my skills. What are your needs?" Parker Palmer had a new book coming out in the fall. Could I help promote it? Terry wondered. I took this to be a sign from God that "way" had opened before me, as the Quakers say. Rush agreed with only a slight slump. With his countless summer trips as a youth pastor, he wouldn't be home much anyway. I couldn't not go.

Rush and I went to counseling a few times leading up to my move—a tune-up, we insisted. As expected, Rush unwittingly charmed our therapist with his glinty eyes and deep laugh, while I was sure I was coming across a pursed-mouth shrew. The men in my life were experts at ingratiating themselves with others, playing sweet to my sour.

"She doesn't like me," I whined to Rush on our way home.

"We don't have to go back," he offered.

After five years of marriage, I worried I was becoming a wife I didn't like and other people pitied. My friend, another pastor's wife, had shaved her head and pierced her nose so that her husband's congregants would know she wasn't domesticated. I wondered if that's what I looked like, acting out some quarter-life crisis and thinking that answers would come with a razor blade or a plane ticket.

I promised Rush that I was moving to Seattle for him just as much as I was doing it for me. "You don't want a wife like this, counting the days until we can move again and start over." I wanted to trust myself, too—trust that I wasn't drifting away. I was going home.

⊟ ⊟ ⊟

We hadn't lived together since high school. But there I was at twenty-seven, saying goodbye to Rush, getting on a plane bound west and moving into my brother's cozy bungalow in Seattle's Central District. All I'd have to cover in rent was the Internet bill for his three roommates.

Charlie met me at the airport in his truck. I ran out of the terminal, threw my bag in the back seat, and leaned over the console to give him a hug. "Can you believe it?" I asked him, my chest ablaze. We drove toward the city, chatting easily, until the skyline came into view, and I felt the first prick of panic. What was I doing here? How would I spend my time? What if I got bored? Worse, what if I loved it? A quick stop in the International District put a food brick over my nascent worry.

My accommodations were sparse. I slept on the floor of his bedroom on a twin mattress, flimsy and yellowed. It was separated from his bed, also on the floor, by a single nightstand with a lamp but no shade. My first day there, Charlie took me down to Value City and let me pick out a new sheet set; I chose a western scene on crisp cotton. A shoe bin from a neighboring curb became my vanity, and the bottom drawer of his dresser served as my closet. I hadn't brought much, mostly sweatshirts and a few casual pants that could pass as professional. Sometimes his friends would pass by our open door and see the setup. "You two living in the same room? I could never do that with my sister."

I didn't always know how to spend my time in the city. Outside of the structured hours of work, I mostly wandered around different neighborhoods and imagined what it would be like to live in the glass-wrapped duplex or the garage apartment with the rusted stairs. Charlie had gotten me a bike off Craigslist to get around. My favorite days were when he'd meet me at the ferry after work, and we'd go riding along the piers, past the touristy seafood restaurants and over to the sculpture garden. When it was time to ride home, I'd ask, "Are we putting our bikes on the bus this time?" It was twenty-two blocks uphill from the wharf to his house. He'd shake his head and smirk, "You can do it."

I had forgotten how much I was capable of on my own. Sure, I was responsible for a hearty portion of the chore wheel growing up. But I also knew how to whine my way out of the most physically exhausting tasks, like scrubbing the bathtub or sponge-painting the basement. When I married Rush, I'd never lived alone before, and while I thought of myself as resourceful, I didn't have to mow the lawn, scrub the dishes or even cut my own toenails now that I had a husband who was eager (and convinced I was lousy at such things). He obliged me in exchange for doing the budget. Charlie was not so accommodating.

My sense of self grew stronger with every pedal. I bought groceries from the local co-op and carried them home on the handlebars of my bike. I cooked meals using real ingredients like fennel and ginger and foraged mushrooms. I attended one of our roommates' jazz concerts all by myself and even rode home in the dark. I jumped off the diving board at Madison Park Beach without plugging my nose. I scoured pans, swept floors and took a taxi to the airport. I stopped cutting my toenails altogether.

I liked myself more than I had in years.

$$\text{⊟ ⊟ ⊟}$$

For a summer, I allowed myself to be a cliché. Instead of regularly going to church, I met God in the hills of the Oregon wine country on a trip with Dad, the crests of Orcas Island with new friends, or the tasty soft-boiled eggs and sriracha mayonnaise Charlie laid out on Sunday mornings. Charlie didn't really go to church anymore—he either worked the early shift at the coffee shop or planned some excursion to Blake Island or Poo Poo Point. The few times we made it to a service on the weekend were flops. Once, I asked him to check out a multiethnic church with me in an industrial part of town. No one talked to us, and we took Communion out of plastic cups. Another time, we visited a charismatic Catholic church up the hill from our house. When it was time for the offering, people processed out of their pews one row at a time to put their money in what looked like a velvet magician's bag. When it was our turn, the usher stood erect next to our pew, and I mistakenly slid my hand across my neck giving him the death sign, instead of the no-thank-you wag. We had nothing to give.

I saw more health in the principles and practices that guided community life at my part-time job than I did at the churches we tried out. "This is what I always thought church would be like," many of our participants reflected when they attended one of our retreats, and I couldn't blame them. Here beliefs were supported with more than just words on a page but in shared touchstones that said *this is how we will belong together*. We received welcome. We turned to wonder. We asked open and honest questions. We listened deeply. We trusted God was housed in each and every one of us.

When I told my roommate Jihi that I worked for an organization with the words *courage* and *renewal* in the title, she said, "Cool, dude. We all need some of that." This kind of secular spirituality was safe and inviting and, for better or worse, optional. She and I and countless others were trying to collect bits and pieces of ourselves out on the left coast. Whether we were from Texas or Delaware, Illinois or North Carolina, we weren't "from here," and there was a certain peace to that. We didn't necessarily want to let our family or religion or region shape us anymore. Some of us had arrived here misshapen and needed to stretch our legs for a while.

35

"I am just so sick and tired of focusing on how depraved I am," I moan and let out a sigh so wide you could stick a fist in it.

"It's Lent, Erin," Rush reasons. "This is precisely the time to focus on where we've gone wrong."

"But we're Easter people!" I rage.

"And it's only six weeks that we remember we haven't always been."

Easter cannot come soon enough this year—and not just because I am fasting from afternoon glasses of Sauvignon Blanc. It's because I feel like I am praying away the screwup in me each time I enter Outpost and have to stare down my shadow once more.

For the past two weeks, I've resolved not to let my decision to eschew membership at Outpost prevent me from going to church altogether. I want to prove that I don't need a set of vows to be held accountable. But it's another set of vows—my marriage vows—that keep me from feeling like I can be fully present there. I wonder if I'm making this harder than it has to be, excuses posing as devotion. I am the one who has a choice, remember; Rush is the one who has a *calling*. No one would blame me for choosing to leave Outpost to be with my husband. They'd praise me for it.

I've been thinking a lot lately about the church where Rush works and the shards it has shot through our home. What were once murmurs of leadership abuse have turned into full-blown charges and disciplinary action against fellow staff members, and he does not know if he can remain there in good faith. He comes home burned out by closed-door meetings, all of the talking and none of the doing. People want to move on, but there are bombs still buried in the sanctuary. It hardly seems time for me to join him in the wreckage.

I feel like telling Lent to get lost this year. I do not want to look back and turn into a pillar of salt. I do not want to make monuments out of my moments of sinfulness. I would rather keep my eyes on the glory by and by. So when Bess emails me asking if I will play an "accuser" at the Tenebrae—or "shadow"—service on Good Friday, I write back, "Yikes!" before agreeing.

⊟ ⊟ ⊟

Between the hours of noon and 3 p.m. on Good Friday, it's common for Catholics to fast in solidarity with the suffering Christ. Many stay home and observe prayerful silence and meditation. If that's too hard, one Catholic website suggests taking up a "particularly unpleasant job which has been put off for a long time—like cleaning the garage or a closet, or scrubbing the bathrooms to emphasize the dreariness appropriate to the day."[5] I consider for a moment if polishing the final pages of a new manuscript proposal might qualify, but before I can make much headway, Perk pulls into the driveway in her hatchback the color of lilac. A small, black hound lunges out of the back seat before Perk can greet me, and just like that, she's running around the yard yelling, "Lucy! Luuucy!"

Perk always arrives in a whirlwind. Eight hours in a car with no one to talk to but the toll collectors on the West Virginia turnpike will do that to you. I help her carry in a parade of small bags: a roller bag of clothes, a tote of dog toys, a fabric purse, a shopping bag, a trash bag and a puffy lunchbox with snacks from the road. She hasn't been in the house for more than five minutes before her laptop comes out of its carrying case and she's showing me pictures of the woman with the freakishly big hands who just moved into her basement.

"Perk, listen to me," I say, swatting her hand away from the keyboard. "We have to leave soon. I agreed to be an accuser at our Tenebrae service and rehearsal starts in a few."

"Am I okay in jeans or should I put on my *leggins*?" She emphasizes the last word as if her "leggins" are the sexiest thing to happen since skorts.

"Your leggings are fine. Just wear something over them that covers your butt."

The sanctuary is quiet when we arrive, the altar bare. Perk asks where the bathroom is, and I shush her. We look around for the other players in the reenactment of Jesus' trial and death. Finally we see a few young adults trickle in and follow them up to the balcony.

Perk and I sit side by side in the pew, awaiting instruction and giggling like schoolgirls. "Can you believe I'm her mom?" she asks when I introduce her, even though I think they can. I ask her if she has any sugar-free gum in her purse, and she starts digging.

"I don't have any individual lines," I tell her, "so you can be an accuser with me, if you want."

"Whatever," she says, pulling out credit cards and coins and lining them up along the tops of her thighs.

Our director, an intense and passionate man, begins the rehearsal and guides us through our scenes. "Project!" he instructs. "Especially you women." He insists it will be powerful for us all as we rehearse the rejection of Christ. "Don't be surprised if the words get caught in your throat."

Perk isn't paying much attention as we go through the script. Her stage whisper is laughable, and it's hard not to give in to her wiles. It isn't until we get to Judas part—the one who betrays Jesus to the authorities—that she sits up in our pew.

"Is Judas here yet?" our director looks around.

Someone shakes his head and mumbles a name, and before I know what's happening, a voice like a foghorn in the darkness shouts, "I'll be Judas!"

It's Perk.

I can't believe it. I can't believe I didn't think of it. I've become so habituated in playing nice at this church that I've hardly been playing myself.

"You can't be Judas," the director quickly admonishes. "Judas needs to be a man."

Now I really can't believe it. I want to growl back, "Well then we might as well kick the white people out of rehearsal for historical accuracy," but I don't because I can be mean when hurt.

"Oh," Perk says, and then lowers her voice a little, "Well, alright." We're no longer laughing by the time the service starts. We play the part of the accusers well, crying, "Crucify him!" from the balcony as we pound our hands into our fists.

He's wrong, though. The words don't get caught in our throat.

☰ ☰ ☰

We're driving home from the service, silent, until Perk wonders aloud what our modern-day "crucify hims" would sound like. What insults do we hurl at the nail-pierced feet of Jesus? I try to think of some really gruesome ones, ones that would make most church folks blush, but when I finally settle on mine, it doesn't sound menacing at all. Still, I know it probably would have crushed him as heavy as those thorns.

"I don't need your church, Lord. I'm all good."

36

There are bad excuses for not joining a church, but there are good ones too, like, "I don't trust their version of God," or "I'm becoming a version of me I don't like." Sometimes the reason is more severe, such as, "The humanity of my neighbors is being systematically threatened here," but often it isn't anybody's fault for the bad match. No one is being malicious or manipulative. The relational dynamics are off. A church whose strength is preaching falls flat on the congregant burnt out on intellectualism. A church whose weakness is diversity wounds deep the congregant hungry to be included.

I've often assumed that if something's hard, it must be worth doing. Call it my own version of the Christian folk wisdom "If the last thing you want to do is be a missionary in Africa, then that's probably what God's calling you to do." I like a challenge. I like to succeed. I like to believe that anything is possible with God and an extra set of hands. This strikes me now as a delusion particular to twenty-somethings but by no means limited to us. Easy is suspicious. Hard is how we prove ourselves. We like to earn merit badges for our perseverance; we think this makes us good, strong, disciplined. Don't get me wrong; the biblical writers are clear throughout Scripture that this life brings suffering. But must we go looking for it?

⊟ ⊟ ⊟

A local legend in Durham, Pauli Murray was raised in a mixed-race family some hundred years ago, her body marked by the violable boundary between slave and slave owner. In her book, *Proud Shoes*, Murray reflected on the place she called home: "Durham was a village without pre–Civil War history or strong ante-bellum traditions. In some ways it was like a frontier town. There was considerable prejudice, of course, but there was recognition of individual worth and bridges of mutual respect between the older white and colored families of the town which persisted into the twentieth century."[6] Reading her words, I wonder if Durham could be considered an outpost for the kingdom too.

A frontier town is an exciting place to be. There are innovators and there are vigilantes. One can make a new name for himself. One can also forget where she came from or who came before her in this strange land. I remember when we first moved to Durham, part of what we liked about the place was how many other transplants lived here. They made us feel less out of place. But so, too, was it comforting to meet long-timers, like Jeanette Stokes, who started the Resource Center for Women in Ministry in the South in 1977 when she was just a few years out of divinity school, or Marcia, who ran the Religious Coalition for a Nonviolent Durham after growing up a race-conscious white girl in Duke Forest during the 1960s. We needed the gifts of these people, too, to show us the way. On the frontier there is a temptation toward rugged individualism on the one hand or native-centric community on the other. It is the same in marriage as we flip flop between arrogantly asserting our will as an individual and passively losing ourselves to the relationship. It is hard to discern a third way.

"Soft individualism" is the term suggested by psychiatrist M. Scott Peck to describe the middle path of belonging. It's the kind of disposition one needs to hold the paradox of self and community. He explains it this way:

> While rugged individualism predisposes one to arrogance, the "soft" individualism of community leads to humility. Begin to appreciate each other's gifts, and you begin to appreciate your own limitations. Witness others share their brokenness, and you will become able to accept your own inadequacy and imperfection. Be fully aware of human variety and you will recognize the interdependency of humanity.[7]

Healthy community, says Peck, is ultimately a realistic community—or to put it another way, a community in which we can be real. I think of my community of college girlfriends, like Jacki and Caroline, who make me feel nothing less than myself when we're together. Words launch from one mouth to the next sound and swift, cheeks flush with laughter and blush with tears, stomachs rock calmly, and minds quiet their analysis. I take space for myself when I need it without worrying I'll be left out. I speak accurately about my life, and in detail, without fear that they'll think I'm bragging or wallowing. I've spazzed and cussed them out and trusted that at the end of it all they'd chalk it up to a blip (or one of my hypoglycemic meltdowns), because they have a whole history of evidence that makes up this sketch of "Erin." I trust their version of me.

It has been harder since living in Durham to find friends who I feel this ease around. I think there's part of me that will always feel a little lost in the South, where bluntness is considered rude and barbecue is considered food. Sometimes it's petty things that leave me feeling left out, like when girlfriends who wear sundresses get more compliments than I do in my boyish, oversized button-downs. Other times it's more distressing, like the unspoken code that we "don't go there" on impolite topics like religion, sexuality or how I've been in a funk since February. I feel sure I've already lost a handful of friends because I haven't been able to swallow my words. "Tell me when this friendship is getting unhealthy," I say to Rush when I come home from yet another coffee date or girls group feeling worse about myself than when I left. We need to regularly ask other people for perspective on where and with whom we come alive; we can't always see things clearly when we're feeling cloudy.

Christians are often cloudy about the distinction between losing our life to Christ and losing one's self in community. Losing our life to Christ means giving up the sin and illusions that alienate us from God. We lose a false life to find the real life (John 10:10). In the same way, a healthy community should help us shed the false selves we've constructed—the facades of pride, privilege and protectiveness that keep us alienated from one another—and uncover the person we are by God's design. Losing one's life should not mean losing all sense of one's self. Instead, in real community we come to find out who it is that we really are, what is it that we can offer and how it is that we belong to this beloved body of believers.

Could I say this honestly about my time at Outpost? Had I been able to receive others' gifts and own my limits? Had I shared in others' vulnerability and accepted my own? Had I seen my fellow congregants and recognized part of myself in them? And if I had, why wasn't this getting any easier?

౾ ౾ ౾

In every community and relationship of which we are a part, we are always discerning the edge of our belonging, that middle place of "soft individualism" where we experience support and challenge, freedom and accountability, unity and diversity. In nature, the edge represents the comingling of two separate but interlocking elements. In his memoir *Soil and Sacrament*, Fred Bahnson writes, "Edge is not so much a place as it is a heightened transfer of energy that happens in the meeting of two distinct entities: field and forest, ocean and estuary, scrub and grassland. These interstitial zones between ecosystems are where the greatest exchanges of life take place."[8] At the edge, the two are softened and transformed.

The exchange of gifts breeds life.

⸗37⸗

Almighty God,

You created us that we might live in you.
You rescued us from sin and death,
And made us alive with Christ,
Joined to him as our head
And to one another as his body.

Yet we move through the world as if we were alone,
Forgetting that we are joined to Christ,
That our life is found in him.
Thinking that we can know and love the Lord
Apart from the fellowship of the church.
And so our schedules and anxieties swirl around our own
Self-evaluation and opportunities
Instead of your call to the church.

When we do gather with your people,
We do not bear with one another as brothers and sisters in Christ.
Instead we interact with each other out of fear.

We allow differences in personality or age,
Culture or education, to obscure the unity of the Spirit.
We fail to believe that you have given gifts to everyone to build up your
*   church.*

So we envy the talents of others.
We deny your generosity toward us,
Focused on self-doubt rather than grateful service.
And so we fail to see your goodness to the least among us,
Accustomed to division
And immaturity in your church,
Instead of seeking to grow up in your love.

Forgive us, Lord, for sins that divide us
From one another
And from you.
Grow us up into the knowledge of your Son
And in submission to him.

Amen.

During Lent, Bess prays these words aloud over the congregation during confession. And for once, instead of speaking aloud only the parts that I think apply to me—a mental game I regularly play of "Yes, I'll confess to that, no, thank you, that's not my sin"—I confess every word.

Lesson Six

OFFERING MY PORTION

To the extent that it is possible,
you must live in the world today
as you wish everyone to live
in the world to come.

ALICE WALKER

Do you really need the church?

So reads the headline of an announcement for a local group called Theology on Tap. My friend Emily forwards me the invitation to the group with a nudge, "Thought you might be interested." Emily is good at belonging—whether to supper clubs or book clubs, neighborhood associations or alumni associations. At twenty-nine, she's even treasurer of something called "garden club" and makes time to visit with women in her neighborhood named Spot and Hopi.

After a year spent trying to belong, I pay attention now to how others give themselves in community. I am an anthropologist of belonging, studying its customs in the lives of friends and strangers. The way a gesture can invite one in. The way language can shut one out. How a habit becomes a feeling and how stillness reveals a truth. Why good icebreakers really do matter.

Debating theology is not really the way to invite belonging. But it is a way to test the truths we're discerning and measure our version of reality against another's. Writing does this too. I suppose it's why I began working on this manuscript before I knew if I could belong to a church now, maybe ever. Can our belonging ever be settled once and for all?

⊟ ⊟ ⊟

With the rise of the religious "nones," there have been countless apologetics for the virtue of being *the* church and, further, the virtue of going to *a* church. Some say church is one of the few public spaces where we come together in regular community to honor body, mind and spirit, but yoga class does that too. Others extol its ability to take us out of our self-centered lives, but a Habitat for Humanity build could do the same. One of the most compelling reasons I've read comes from Chaplain Tara Woodard-Lehman, who says she needs church because she has a bad memory. She writes:

> I need Church, because Church reminds me of everything that's important. And when I say Church, I'm not talking about a building. I mean the people. I'm referring to the organic, collective, flesh and blood Body of Christ. I'm talking about the beautiful but undeniably imperfect community of people who help me remember who I am, and to Whom I belong, over and over again.[1]

Sitting across a picnic table at the local brewery, Perry, a divinity student here in Durham, tells us he needs church to remember too. But it's not primarily the preaching of the Christian story that rekindles his memory, nor the presence of the people in the pew that reminds him why he is there. "It's the Eucharist that gets me out of bed on Sunday morning," he says.

It's the sacrament that reminds him he belongs.

I like his answer. The sacraments are not first things we commit to doing but gifts we prepare to receive. This is the harder lesson for people like me who want to work for our belonging, want the challenge of being chosen. God's gifts are almost too good to be true. Tertullian wrote of the sacraments, "There is nothing which so hardens men's hearts as the contrast between the simplicity apparent in the performance of God's works and the grandeur promised as their eventual outcome."[2] It bothers us, I think, that the sacraments are so simple to procure: baptism requires only tap water; the Eucharist, wheat and grapes; marriage, a piece of paper. But something happens when the ordinary elements of earth join with the extraordinary promises of God. Our world becomes joined with God's kingdom. Our relationships become a reflection of God's communion. Our belonging becomes bound to God's household. Our reality expands.

If the sacraments remind us that the promises of God spoken

throughout Scripture are available for us to receive, I still wonder why I don't always experience their power in the local church. Why do I not taste belonging when I walk into a sanctuary on Sunday morning and scoot silently into a pew? Where is its peace when I am listening to a sermon in which I find nothing of my story in the story of us? How is it that a congregation can ask me to commit to its beliefs before it knows any of mine? Is the unity of the faith witnessed at Pentecost realistic when there are still so many who do not thrive as full human beings in the institution of the church?

At Theology on Tap, we pass around an open bag of Trader Joe's pirate booty and leave the veggies untouched. We share ourselves and our stories of why we need the church, and when it gets to me, I bury my hands under me and lean back. It is time to test my truth.

"I need the church to remind me what's real."

In 1975, Reverend Bill Hybels started Willow Creek Community Church in a rented movie theater. It's now one of the largest and most widely recognized churches in America. While its mission to "turn irreligious people into fully devoted followers of Jesus Christ" has remained the same for decades, the driving question of a new generation of faith seekers has changed. "Thirty years ago, we argued about what was true," Hybels said in an interview. "These days, people seem to be asking, 'What's real?'"[3]

What's real? It's a question too big to answer but too big not to try. With so many sectors competing to sell us their version of reality— science and self-help, technology and sociology, politics and Hollywood—it's more vital than ever that the church serves as a threshing place for its members to sort illusion from reality, fiction from truth, death dealers from life givers. How we do this will depend on the different emphases our communities put on things like Scripture, sacraments and how God speaks. But it starts with each of us getting real. We need to get real about what we believe and then ask what practices support those beliefs.

Do we really believe that we each have gifts worth offering one another? Then let's make a gifts inventory representing all the people in our church so you know I like giving rides to doctor appointments and I know you are willing to offer free counseling. At our church in Berkeley, we had an expectation that each member of the congregation would be involved in "worship + 2": worship + small group + service opportunity. If we each have something to give, then we each need to be regularly nurturing and using our gifts alongside one another.

Do we really believe that vulnerability is a risk we're called to take? Then let's establish some ground rules for how we will create safe space when we're together. For example, we could agree to speak only for ourselves when sharing personal experiences in small groups and to hold off judgment, counsel or compassionate commiseration unless asked. In order to create safe space on Courage & Renewal retreats, we also maintain something called "double confidentiality" in groups where someone is discerning an important question about life or work. Double confidentiality means that we agree not to share what's been said with those outside the group, and we also agree not to bring up what's been said to the person who shared it at some later date. We trust people to speak their need if they want to talk further, rather than trying to anticipate it for them.

Do we really agree that there's value in inviting strangers into our midst? Then let's make it a relational norm that we wear name tags during worship, pass the peace first to someone we didn't come with, or build in time for a spontaneous meal after worship. And, good Lord, can we actually make a bulletin that could be followed by a newcomer? One of the things I appreciate most at Outpost is their weekly practice of asking us to sign our names on a pad of paper at the end of the pew. This isn't chiefly for the higher-ups "to know you were here" but rather to help the people in the pews learn the names of fellow worshipers. It also puts the responsibility on those of us who have been around longer to shake hands with first-time visitors rather than waiting for a church staff member to follow up later. We are the laity; hospitality is our work.

Do we really agree that we should treat one another charitably? Then let's host a storytelling night in which we can test our truths with civility; my friend Dani regularly organizes something like this for ReImagine, a spiritual formation center in San Francisco. Instead of initiating a debate about theology or theory, she picks a theme and invites a handful of people from different backgrounds to prepare a story connected to that theme and reflect on how it's shaped their faith identity. Our stories are entryways into discussing how we've come to believe as we do without arguing in abstractions but finding connection in the details. Frederick Buechner wrote, "It is precisely through these stories in all their particularity, as I have long believed and often said, that God makes himself known to each of us more powerfully and personally."[4]

Do we really agree that earnestness is more important than rightness? Then let's act like we believe Jesus' words that "whoever is not against us is for us" (Mark 9:40). Let's let go of our suspicion of those Christians or those atheists not like us and cultivate a healthy curiosity about the world from their vantage. Do we think they have something of worth to offer us in our small group studies, sermon series and liturgies? Do we think attending their yoga workshop or prayer rally is worth our time? Do we think we will look foolish if we're too welcoming, too permissive, too indiscriminate? If they are living the good news in spirit but not in name, then they are fellow cocreators of the reality we long to make known.

When I was in college, my drama professor once said to me, "Erin, do you really believe that belief in Jesus is the key to eternal life?"

I responded that I did.

"Eternal life?" he asked again.

Yes, I know. It sounded ridiculous for a twenty-one-year-old to presume such a thing, but yes, I believed that life with Jesus was better than any life we could know apart from him.

"Then why aren't you out there every day knocking down doors? If you think you know *the key to eternal life*, why aren't you fumbling over yourself to share this news with the world?"

He had a point. Nevermind my introversion or demanding class schedule, my actions didn't support my belief that real life was available and abundantly made known in Christ.

People figure this out about us Christians. They figure out that we don't always do what we mean or mean what we say. That's okay if we can admit as much and continue to realign ourselves with our values. When I ask my Dad what he thinks of his current priest, he says, "I don't feel like he's a real person." Real people aren't perfect. They're honest. They don't speak in buzz words like "grace" or "mission" or "holiness," but they spell out what they mean and why they mean it and sometimes even what it might mean for us. It's why Pope Francis is so beloved around the world; his kind of common-sense Christianity of humble living, indiscriminate blessing and condemnation of the abuse of power actually resembles the ministry of Jesus. The logical correlation between belief and actions, along with genuine humility, is what builds trust. When it's missing, authenticity gets traded for illusion.

What makes the church toxic then is not its ability to leave us feeling disillusioned. Disillusionment, remember, is what the cross is all about. What makes the church toxic is when it crafts the very illusions it should be unmasking. When the church weaves the illusion of scarcity, we say, "There is not enough time or money or members for us to survive. We must try harder." When we believe the illusion of separation, we tell ourselves, "It's easier to take care of our own needs than admit our need for each other. We must not appear weak."

When we wield the illusion of control, we act as if making our world small will keep our church safe. We must shut mystery out. When we spew the illusion of difference, we act as if the heavenly reality of equality is not meant to be imaged in the earthly realities of marriage, politics and the pulpit. We must behave.

Then there's the illusion that prompted this journey one year ago when I confessed, "I want to belong but don't know how." When we believe the illusion of alienation, we're prone to treating belonging as a privilege earned rather than a gift offered.

I don't have to travel far from home for my last Courage & Renewal retreat. It's just a few hours in the car from Durham to the interfaith retreat center where we'll be gathering. Rush has been out of town on a mission trip for a few days, and I'm eager to hear myself talk aloud again. I take care to vacuum Amelia's hair out of the car and pick up two dozen mini cupcakes downtown before leaving. Through an unruly email chain of exclamation marks and emoticons, we've all agreed to bring our favorite food from home to share.

On my way, I stop in Greensboro to pick up Mary Ellen, Al and Barbara at the International Civil Rights Center & Museum; they are tickled to have run into a few of the aging activists who performed a sit-in at the Woolworth's department store counter in 1960. Barbara doesn't mind sitting with the cupcakes on her lap in the front seat, and I give Al my bag of almonds and blueberries. He's forgotten to eat today.

I've heard it takes, on average, about seventeen hours for a group to bond. I suppose this is why youth groups like Rush's do overnight Harry Potter marathons or weeklong hiking trips on the Appalachian Trail. It takes time, lots of time, to not just *live* like we belong but *feel* like we belong to one another. One consulting book I read suggests churches have two tracks for membership; a quick route for those who don't have a lot of questions (read angst) and a longer period of discernment for those like me who have an unending appetite for reflection and a community of practice.[5] In the Quaker tradition, prospective members request a "clearness committee" in which they gather with a small group of longtime congregants to recount their journey to belonging over the course of a few hours. The process is often a formal recognition of a reality long felt rather than a test of one's allegiance.[6] It is not a one-time decision or a five-class commitment but an ongoing process by which one matures into the fullness of belonging.

At our final retreat together, we each prepare a practice session to lead for a small group of colleagues. We relish how each facilitator puts his or her own spin on the timeless principles and practices that define our work. An elementary schoolteacher leads her small group through a wine-tasting experience with the theme of "savoring the moment." A Baptist preacher plays Sam Cooke's "A Change Is Gonna Come" to lead us in a meditation on hope. I choose a poem from St. Francis of Assisi about the reality-making power of the stories we tell.

By the last night, we have been together this past year for a total of 270+ hours if you count the time we were separated only by sleep. We dance to celebrate. We dance on the back patio of the retreat center while the preacher holds his phone up in the air and plays Beyoncé. Mukta shows me her "screw in the light bulb" move, and I joke to Kelly—the only other facilitator my age—that I have been parodying other people's dance moves for so long I think they're my own now. Sue passes around organic chocolate bars from Portland, and Al brings out a bag of cheese curds from Wisconsin.

This is how belonging happens. Not by waiting for permission or holding out for perfect conditions. Not by cherry-picking people just like us or nitpicking people who don't get us. Belonging happens when we choose to give ourselves away, saying, "Take. Eat. If you'll have me, I belong to you."

When I began writing this book, I was surprised to find that there's no one word for belonging in the New Testament. The Greek word most commonly associated with modern translations is rendered *este*, which means "are, is or be."[7] Often we see this word in Paul's writing as a possessive article. For instance, when we read, "You belong to Christ" (1 Corinthians 3:23), the more wooden translation is "You are of Christ." In this way we might think of parents sitting side by side at a peewee soccer game, asking, "Which one is yours?" It reminds us we belong to God not because of anything we do but because of who we are.

In the Old Testament, however, there's a word for belonging that's more concrete. The Hebrew noun for belonging is rendered *manah*, and it refers to the part or portion in a sacrificial offering that belongs to us.[8] "And thou shalt take the breast of the ram of Aaron's consecration, and wave it for a wave offering before the Lord: and it shall be thy *part*" (Exodus 29:26 KJV, emphasis added). In the book of Esther, we see the word show up again in the command to celebrate the festival of Purim whereby the Jews joyfully send their *portions* of the sacrificial meal to one another and the poor (Esther 9:22). Belonging to God compels us to share our offering in community. But the most interesting part of the word *manah* is that we do not get to choose what our offering will be; it comes assigned or ordained to us by God. The offering is our true selves. It's as if God says, "There's no use trying to play someone else. Your part is worthy. Now go, offer your portion faithfully."

I'd had it wrong all along. Belonging didn't chiefly depend on whether a community accepted me but whether I was able to offer myself to them. Isn't this the way God chose to belong to us? God recognized that even with loving commandments and specific regulations and a land marked promise, we weren't able to accept God's affection. And so God sent his only Son, Jesus Christ, as the ultimate offering and said, "Take. Eat. If you'll have me, I belong to you." Offering ourselves in community is not only the response to our belonging in Christ but the seal.

We seal our belonging with one another on our last retreat together as we share music from our iPods and food from our homes. We each offer our part, and accept each other's with thanks and awe. Some of us dance, some of us sit, and some of us go back to our rooms early. I keep dancing.

= 41 =

It's Easter Sunday, and I make Perk get to Outpost twenty minutes early. This is the Catholic in me, the one who used to get dropped off in front of the sanctuary to "go grab seats" only to find herself and her family relegated to the fellowship hall where the misfits and latecomers were punished by the cold, hard bottoms of folding chairs. At this Presbyterian congregation we have our pick of the pews.

Perk wants to sit on the side, near the back, and so she shimmies down a row and drops her purse on the floor. I slide in beside her. Minutes later, she is rummaging through her belongings, pulling out wandering coins and foil wrappers.

"Excuse me, honey bun," she says and stands to exit.

"Bathroom again?" I ask.

"No. I want to take a picture of the altar. It's so pretty."

"Mom, no one takes pictures in church."

"Oh, Erin," she says and pushes past my legs into the aisle.

I watch her approach the front of the sanctuary. There's a wooden table with a water jug on it. She takes a few pictures from different angles, even walks around the pulpit and kneels for a better shot at one point. The whole scene looks rather plain to me. She must see something I don't.

Our associate pastor Rob is giving the sermon today. He preaches on Jesus' postresurrection walk to Emmaus. The story begins as two followers of Jesus start out on a journey of seven miles. At some point, we don't exactly know when, Jesus joins them—or "came near" (Luke 24:15). They are deep in discussion, probably playing and replaying the events of the past few days—betrayal, death and a missing body—like it's something out of one of those crime dramas Perk watches. When Jesus comes near, they are trying to make sense of what is real and what is spiritual smoke.

He appears a stranger to them at first. They fill him in on the drama, how they had hoped Jesus of Nazareth was the Savior, the one Israel had been waiting for, but now it has been *three whole days* and there's been nothing more than reports from some fanatical women about an empty tomb. Jesus can stand their nonsense no more. He calls them slow of heart—slow of heart to believe the new reality. That he has risen. That they are saved. That it is finished.

But this isn't my favorite part of the story. Not even close.

When the disciples reach their destination, they turn off the road, maybe even with an awkward, "Well, this is us," unsure if Jesus will continue on with them—*wants* to continue on with them—or has better things to do. And Jesus, Rob points out, instead of following them, instead of continuing to convince them with his divine interpretation of events, "walked ahead as if he were going on" (Luke 24:28). Did you get that? Jesus pretends to keep going, ahead, onward, by himself. But why? Some scholars say he does it to give the disciples an opportunity to practice hospitality,[9] but I think it's something more basic. I think it's about longing.

In offering himself as bread for the world, Jesus ran the risk of being rejected, and he was by many who wanted no part in his part. There's no guarantee our offerings to the world will be received any better. There's nothing to say someone will accept our gifts, handle them with care or help them come alive. But it's our choice to offer them. It's in the offering that we accept belonging for ourselves.

The disciples don't want their time with Jesus to end. So they urge him to come with them. They invite him to their table. "Stay with us," they say. One wonders if this was what Jesus was hoping for all along. Was it his ploy to continue on in holy passive aggressiveness, whereby Jesus, like a beleaguered spouse, thought, "I know what *I* want you to do, but I want *you* to do it without my asking"? Or is it possible the Savior of the universe is longing to belong to us?

Before there were dollars and cents and twenty-something artisans peddling their wares on the website Etsy, the gift economy was the central means by which communities achieved peace both within and between neighboring tribes. A gift rightly offered and fittingly exchanged could prevent not just internal turmoil but war between tribes. In his essay "The Spirit of the Gift," twentieth-century anthropologist Marshall Sahlins reflects on how all gifts bear the goal of reconciliation. He quotes a Bushman as having said: "We give what we have. That is the way we live together."[10]

We give what we have. This is also the way we worship together. In the economy of the local church, we are reconciled to one another by need, both our need to receive the gifts of one another, but so too the need to feel like we have something of worth to give. It isn't enough to just speak our need. We need to feel needed in return.

The more I've thought about it, the more I believe belonging is a two-way street, not a tit-for-tat contract that asks what we each get out of this but a covenantal relationship by which promises are made and gifts are exchanged. So in addition to asking, *Do I really need the church?* we should also be asking, *Does the church really need me?* or *How is it that we belong by our longing for each other?*

I find it strange that membership in many churches across America has more to do with an individual's commitment to the worshiping community rather than the other way around. If there are promises made by the congregation, they are often universal and abstract, having little to do with the gifts and personalities of the ones they are being promised to. Perhaps this is my "everybody deserves a medal" millennialism speaking, but I want it to matter that I, Erin Lane, grade-A awkward at belonging, introverted, critical and sensitive human being, am joining this local body of believers. I need to believe that I am not just another sack of bones in this congregation, just another number to report to the denomination's judicatory board, just another person to "plug in" somewhere so that this church can survive. God may choose to include Jew and Gentile alike in the new covenant of bread and cup, but God also chooses each one of us by name.

If I am to join a church, any church, maybe even your church, I need to believe that you want *me* to belong. This me. The me that I will be in a week. The me that is always arriving. And when this me pretends to walk away, go on ahead, forge the path by herself, I need you to say the following words with some sense of urgency:

"Stay with us."

And I will try.

It's been said that those most in love with the church have the hardest time belonging to it. John O'Donohue calls this type of moody and intense lover of tradition the artist. We often think of artists as living on the edge of culture, the innovators and free thinkers, but O'Donohue describes the artist this way: "He inhabits the tradition to such depth that he can feel it beat in his heart, but his tradition also makes him feel like a total stranger who can find for his longing no echo there."[11] Artists live on the edge not of culture but of heartbreak. We are the faithful rebels.

One month after Easter, the pastors begin a sermon series at Outpost on the patriarchs of the faith. Every week since I decided not to join this church, I have shown up, stubborn and resolved, to belong to this community in practice if not in name. I want to show them. I want to show myself. I am not bad at this.

It's a small thing, I tell myself, to have to sit through another sermon on the God of Abraham, Isaac and Jacob; I remind myself this is my God too. But this one small thing has been added to many small things; a hairline fracture that, if left untreated, could break me one day when I least expect it. I've told myself before that of all the things the early church discerned as essential to the faith a gender-balanced view of God and God's people was not one of them. I've also told myself that the church witness has been on the wrong side of history more than once; tradition is a living thing. So you disagree with tradition? It's okay. You can stay, Erin. You can settle your dispute and discern a new word. You can be human. There are other humans here too.

My tongue gets the better of me one Sunday. It's Pentecost Sunday again, and I am reminded how often I feel like the adopted child in this male-dominated tradition. I try to be more charitable in my thoughts but I wince when Martin describes the "Jesus who looked like a carpenter's son," when it wasn't even that carpenter that gave him life. What of Mary's boy? I will have to eventually speak up if this is the place where I intend to offer not just my gifts but my heartbreak too. On my way out the door, I quip to Martin, "I look forward to hearing your next sermon series on the matriarchs."

As soon I say it, I'm sorry. He doesn't need that kind of pastoral whiplash. I get on my bike and ride. The whole way home I work over my comment like a woman punching dough. I shouldn't have said it. Punch. Or should I? Punch. Was I losing it? Was I losing my sanity by saying something? Stop punching. Or my dignity by not saying anything at all? Punch. Punch. Punch. It's hard to sort it out alone.

When I sit down at the computer to write for the afternoon, I can't think straight. I pause. I breathe. I write an email instead.

Dear Martin,
When I think about my experience at Outpost this past year, I'm re-
minded of a line in an old Negro spiritual: "Sometimes I feel like a

motherless child. A long ways from home." Like an adopted child into a tradition largely passed on through the writing of men, I long for the stories of my birth mothers to be lifted up—from Eve to Sarah to Esther to Ruth to Mary to Julian to Dorothy to the women who surround me now.

When I sit in those pews and hear nothing of them, nothing of me, it makes me feel small in the unholiest of ways, and I'm left jumping hurdles in my imagination to believe that I really belong here, that this is really what "kingdom come" looks like for all of us.

I don't believe you or anyone else at Outpost intends to alienate me. And I have enough theological knowledge to know that men aren't the only pillars in our tradition. That when we talk about Abraham, we are talking about Sarah and Hagar. When we talk about Moses, we are talking about the twelve women in the first book of Exodus who paved the way out. When we talk about David, we are talking about Ruth. When we talk about Jesus, we are talking about Mary. When we talk about the Spirit, we are talking about Wisdom. I know this, and yet it is lonely to know it without hearing it spoken aloud in community.

I'm grateful for your listening ear. I hope your time on sabbatical is rich with all sorts of new learning and creativity and discipline. When you return, I hope we can meet in person again and catch up. Thanks for who you are and what you do in this place.

Warmly,
Erin

I mean it. I mean those words when I write them. I believe Martin means it, too, when he responds, "I look forward to talking about these matters, which matter." But he goes on sabbatical for the summer and when he returns we don't catch up. I don't initiate. He doesn't initiate. I convince myself we both have better things to do.

After a little more than a year, I can no longer say I don't know how to belong. I recently heard a prominent theologian suggest that repetition brings God delight. Richard Mouw, former president of Fuller Theological Seminary, told the story of his grandson who loves to see his old 'pa make funny faces. He obliges and the little boy claps and spits with glee. "Do it again!" he screams. This, Mouw suggested, is something of the delight God takes in us. In our waking, our breakfast making, our laboring, our evening praying, God says, "That's good. Do it again." This is the rhythm of commitment. We name our desire in earnestness. We test our ability to trust. We show up and shake hands. We risk speaking our need. We discern the shape of our gifts and whether or not we want to offer them in this particular community. In this way, we rehearse not only the knowledge of *how* to belong but also the knowledge *that* we belong.

Belonging may be a reality already promised to us by God, but so too is it a reality we participate in, claiming for ourselves and others as we make decisions again and again about where and with whom to offer our presence. There will come a time when we will know God fully even as we are fully known, a time when we will understand God's people even as we are understood, a time when there will be no painful contradictions between reality as it should be and reality as we know it. Until that time, faithful rebels must learn to live at the edge not just of our own heartbreak, but of this world and the world to come.

≡ ≡ ≡

An increasing number of folks my age are choosing to live on the edge of belonging; we may not be fully in or fully out, but we are not "nones." In an article on faith and leadership, Reverend Dori Baker reflects on a pilgrimage she took in 2013 to commemorate the fiftieth anniversary of the March on Washington. She noted, "The young leaders I journeyed with [didn't] see the borders, the divisions, the walls, the pews or the collection plates. In fact, they are drawn to the edges between race, ethnicity, gender, sexual orientation, worship style, denomination, cherished biblical passages, paid work and volunteerism."[12] Old labels are wearing thin, their edges curling up on our breasts like name tags that have lost their stick.

Even the labels of being "affiliated" or "unaffiliated" with the church strike me as silly for those who follow the teachings of Jesus. (Research has shown that even within the category of the "nones," there is a distinction between "secular nones" and "liminal nones," the latter of whom have some on-again, off-again relationship with a faith community. To complicate the label even further, one-third of all liminal nones even identify as belonging to a congregation!)[13] A Christian can no more be unaffiliated with the church than the nose can be unaffiliated with the toes. The apostle Paul put it this way: "If the ear should say, 'Because I am not an eye, I do not belong to the body,' it would not for that reason stop being part of the body" (1 Corinthians 12:16 NIV). Sure, some Christians may choose not to attend a church, may choose to ignore the tradition, may choose to migrate West in order to start fresh without the trappings of religion, but we are still a part of the body of Christ. We are still the heartbeat of Jesus' own longing when he prays, "That they may be one, as we are one" (John 17:22).

I don't know what the Christian church in America will look like in twenty, thirty, fifty years as my generation tests our millennial ideals with experience. Some say denominations are a thing of the past; the house church will replace the megachurch; the priesthood of all believers will replace the priest; participation will replace affiliation. Robert P. Jones of the Public Religion Research Institute describes the impact of our shifting allegiances:

> I think the days of standing in the pulpit looking out in the pews in a Presbyterian church or a Methodist church and thinking most of these people in here are cradle-to-grave are gone. More than three in 10 Americans are switching their religious affiliation at least once—and I don't just mean Methodist to Presby-

terian. I mean Catholic to mainline Protestant or Muslim to Buddhist. They're big switches, not just denominational trades.[14]

Questions of belonging—how it's fostered and how it's discerned—are questions that will only grow in importance as we rethink old realities and risk living into ones yet seen.

While denominationalism continues to have little significance to me and many of my peers, there's one commitment I won't give up: the local church. The church is a package deal with belief in Christ; we are an unavoidable trinity of belonging—me, you and God. Members of one another rather than an institution, Christians are meant to regularly gather and practice our belonging as civil, compassionate and cross-bearing citizens of the world. If our church is not a safe space where all can show up with thin skin, then it is we who have work to do in co-creating the most logical reality of all: "Thy kingdom come . . . on earth as it is in heaven" (Matthew 6:10 RSV).

⊟ ⊟ ⊟

To live like we belong to the body of Christ requires the ability to hold many contradictions. Even in the structure of the word *belonging* itself we recognize that we have to figure out a way to *be* present in our current community while embracing our *longing* for change.

I think many young people have found no echo for our longing in the church, not because we don't care but because we care so much it hurts. It is not out of irreverence that we rebel against committing to the church and all of the unattractive words that come with it like *submission* and *accountability*. It is out of our reverence that we call it to higher ways, to be a better version of itself, a more creative representation of reality as we know it. I know it's audacious to believe that I or anyone else knows what's more real than the next glimpse. But I'd wager we've all caught glimpses of the heavenly reality with our own eyes. Those moments when we know in our flesh and bone that this,

this is the kingdom come. This, this is why with we groan in *earnestness* to make it so, on earth as it is heaven.

The problem is, it's hard to call the church out when we're not faithfully under its shelter. "If you're not part of the solution, you're part of the problem" was a popular saying from the 1960s. It's all wrong, though, when it comes to the most meaningful way change happens, says Bill Torbert. "The slogan should be, 'If you're not part of the problem, you can't be part of the solution.'"[15] If we want the church to be a place where we no longer feel like strangers, we need to take ownership for the ways our actions—and our inability to belong—have made it harder for others like us to find their home there. It's why when earnest, edge-dwelling people tell me they don't go to church, I get sort of down (after a brief and misguided reaction of, No fair!). You are the people with whom I need to come together and mature my faith. We are the people who are part of the problem.

Each of us has a choice in how we will respond to our heartbreak. We can either let it take us out of the action in favor of a simpler life where we belong without question or question without belonging, or we can let it lead us into a more vibrant life in which the contradictions of our faith open us to the death of illusions, the suffering of community and the resurrection of our real selves. Parker Palmer calls this latter option the "broken-open heart" and says hearts such as these are the strength of every generation that has sought to call forth an alternative reality of hope.[16]

At the beginning of summer, I wrote to Martin, "Sometimes I feel like a motherless child. A long ways from home." The contradiction between longing and belonging is still one of the most confounding parts of the Christian tradition to me. We somehow both already belong to the household of God and yet we wander about like strangers with home-shaped holes in our hearts. I used to think that longing for home was for middle-schoolers with separation anxiety—a nameless ache we grow out of over time as we make homes of our own. Now I see that homesickness is our spiritual condition. Even our ancestors Abraham and Sarah are described in the book of Hebrews as strangers still longing for "a better country" (Hebrews 11:16.) They are *still* longing for a better reality. Even now. Even after they're gone. And they long not out of some childish coping mechanism but as a sign of their faith, faith that the heaven on earth whispered about long ago is real but takes some *getting to*, some *working out*, some *traveling toward*.

May our longing lead us home.

EPILOGUE

The mosquitoes are beginning to leave us in September. I open the door a little further on the screened porch now. Amelia sits next to me and yawns, pulling her tongue back into the cavern of her mouth. My Bible is laid out on my lap, and I am praying. Or thinking. I cannot tell the difference when Rush opens the back door of the house with a look of urgency.

"I have an interesting proposition for you," he says, putting his workbag on the couch beside me. "But I can come back. I mean, if you were praying or something and want me to come back. Were you praying?"

I close my Bible. "I don't think so. Maybe. Anyway, what is it?"

His eyes grow wider, his pupils pulsing. Ever since the bishop appointed a new senior pastor to his church in September, he's been coming home talking about youth retreats and mission outreach instead of conflict mediations. His vision has returned and it reaches farther afield than either one of us thought possible three months ago.

"It's a red truck. Jim wants to get a new car for Jack before he goes off to college, so he's selling his truck and putting it on eBay tomorrow morning, unless, uh, unless we make him an offer first."

I've always dreamed of owning a truck as our second car. Even before Charlie got a truck, I wanted one, I swear. Most trucks can't fit more than me, Rush and Amelia in the cab, but there's plenty of room to lug our camping gear for a quick weekend away or carry a friend's furniture across town to her new apartment. A truck meant we were ready for anything, up for anything. Available for whoever needs us, wherever the Spirit sends us.

It feels important to practice the ministry of availability, especially as friends like Juli and Corey prepare to welcome their first baby into the world and turn their attention toward making a home of their own for a while. Taylor and Blair left our small group over the summer, their time full enough with commitments to their burgeoning careers and Taylor's burgeoning belly. Last month, in the chocolate aisle at a health-food market, Bess tells me she is pregnant too. When everyone was moving across the country finding love and switching jobs and collecting degrees, mobility seemed more like a liability to relationships than an asset. Now, as friends slow their pace and find their place, I wonder about the gift I might offer to my community by not being quite as attached, quite as settled, quite as rooted as all the others.

I see my marriage differently too these days. I returned home from Seattle two years ago more sure of myself, which made me more sure of Rush. It's funny how that happened. There's a new kind of freedom I'm learning that comes not from keeping my options open but from choosing the life in front of me (as long as it's in front of me). Now Rush and I have started asking, What if our mutual desire for a life without biological kids reveals a gift, rather than a fear? Maybe it isn't just a coincidence or lack of confidence that brought two people together who didn't think pregnancy was one of those must-have experiences of life. Rush loves being with other people's kids, and I'm eager to invite more strangers into our lives, including strange children and their strange network of families, social workers and lawyers. Over the summer I even made it to a foster-parent support group that meets regularly at Outpost.

Although Martin and I haven't communicated since his return from sabbatical in August, I continue to look for other allies in belonging here. Georgia thinks my facilitation skills might be of some use in training small group leaders for the fall women's retreat, and even though at first blush this might seem like the last thing I'd want to do, I think I have something to offer. We're planning a meal at Georgia's house later this month where I'll fuse some of our Courage & Renewal touchstones for creating safe space with passages from Scripture. I'll be sure to make name tags.

"What are we talking here for this truck?" I ask. "$5,000? $10,000?"

"Something like that. I didn't ask how much he was listing it for," Rush says.

This is so unlike Rush. I am the dreamer; he's the pragmatist. We have always been good together this way, course correcting each other's view of reality—mine often impossibly idealistic, his often depressingly realistic. It is one of the greatest surprises in our marriage of seven years that Rush has become more adventurous in spirit while I have sought more solid ground. I find myself using words I would have recoiled at five years earlier, words like *sustainability* or *longevity*. I wonder whether we should buy another cheap rug from Target or splurge for a patchwork one from that shop in downtown Durham. I save old bedding and old furniture in the off chance that we'll finish the attic someday and give foster kids a room of their own. I wonder if we do welcome kids in five, ten, fifteen years, if it makes sense to continue attending churches apart. And if it doesn't make sense then, I wonder why it makes sense now.

I curl my legs beneath me on the couch, folding in on myself while I think. "Do you want to offer something? I guess what I'm asking is, is it really worth thousands of dollars to be able to worship together every Sunday?"

He laughs. "When you put it that way I don't know if the answer is obviously yes or obviously no."

Neither do I.

All I know in the moment is this: there is a red truck for sale, and I like picturing myself in it.

The wind blows where it chooses, and you hear the sound of it, but you do not know where it comes from or where it goes. So it is with everyone who is born of the Spirit.

JOHN 3:8-9

ACKNOWLEDGMENTS

God, pardon the cheese factor here, but the first shout-out goes to you. Do you remember when I first got the offer to write this book five years ago from another publisher? Of course you do; you remember everything. So you'll also remember that they eventually said never mind, and so I said never mind too, for a while until I regained my confidence. You are my confidence. In the spirit of Elizabeth who prayed for a baby as I prayed for this book, I say, "This is the Lord's doing."

Jonathan, you're next in the line-up because you're next in the timeline and my brain is too tired after a year and a half of writing to think nonlinearly. When we sat down for coffee, you with your Mickey Mouse mug, me with my paper cup, you told me to write a book proposal in thirty days or less and just be done with it. I needed that Holy Spirit kick. Thanks, too, for reading my stuff and treating me like I belonged among writers.

Enuma, Jason and Sheryl: I still pinch myself that you consider me a friend. You read my proposal and told me you'd want to read this book, and I believed you, because (maybe I shouldn't tell you this) I believe almost everything you say. You helped me be smart with my art, skimpy on the snark and true to my heart. Let's all hang out someday.

Then there's Nick who introduced me to Dave who introduced me to the whole InterVarsity Press team. Dave, let me say this, I wouldn't have signed with IVP if it weren't for your assurance that Crescendo was about lifting up women authors and not "the woman experience." You've left me in the hands of good women—Cindy, Lorraine, Alisse, Leah, Adrianna, Krista and countless others behind the scenes.

To Katie, who read my manuscript through one more time for me when I was freaking out. Every writer needs a writer friend like you who makes reassuring comments in the margins and knows the difference between character Erin, narrator Erin and the real deal. You're the real deal.

To Juli and Corey. You two are some kind of friends. Juli, you are as wise as you are kind; I couldn't have written this book without your help as a researcher, proofreader and all around cheerleader. Corey, you wear your heart on your sleeve and remind me to do the same, even when I'm fried or in a mood. In fact, you both make me feel like my moods are kind of charming. Bless you.

To Mom and Dad, for never, ever, ever saying, "Because I said so." You gave me the gift of curiosity. And then you gave me another gift when you said I had carte blanche to write about you. Charlie, I couldn't be a part of this fearless family without you. You will always feel like home to me.

Rush, I already sort of thanked you in the dedication so I feel like it would be a little greedy of you to expect something more here. If I were to say something more, though, it would be this: you are a saint. You are so much of a saint that your one critique of the book was that I made you look like a saint. Who, other than a saint, would say such a saintly thing? Who, other than a saint, would read my book through twice in print, hear it read once out loud and sit through many an impromptu conversation on "option A" or "option B"? I choose you.

FOR REFLECTION

Lesson 1: The Importance of Being Earnest

1. A group of middle schoolers made a distinction between fitting in and belonging. Describe a time when it was clear you were trying to fit it. Now describe a time when you experienced a sense of belonging. How do *you* discern the difference?

2. What illusions keep you from feeling a sense of belonging with the church? In this first section, Erin names the illusion of difference, feeling "other" than *those* Christians; the illusion of control, that productivity on Sunday is more important than presence; and the illusion of alienation, that it isn't in her nature to belong.

3. In the past, how did you know when you'd found "the one"— church or partner? What were you looking for? What did you find? What, if anything, was "earnest" about your search?

Lesson 2: The Art of Reading Charitably

1. The cynic believes that there can be no new possibilities, only a rehearsal of what has already been. In what relationship in your life do you doubt change can happen? Who in your life do you want to practice charity toward?

2. "Opposition," John O'Donohue wrote, "forces our abilities to awaken; it tests the temper and substance of who we are." Have you experienced opposition as a gift in your relationship with the church? Why or why not?

3. What might it mean for you to believe that trust is something that happens *with* you rather than *to* you? Name one or two things that you might start doing differently if you actually believed this.

Lesson 3: The Discipline of Showing Up

1. What does it mean to go to church "past the point of feeling and into the realm of habit"? Erin names a few habits—like regularly showing up at worship, accepting invitations and learning the names of strangers. What habits help you sustain your involvement at church?

2. What did your parents, teachers, church, etc., teach you about strangers growing up? Tell a story about a time you interacted with a stranger that has been formational—positive or negative—in your faith journey.

3. How did you get your name? What do your parents call you? What does God call you? What do you like to call yourself? How does your name make you feel like you do or don't belong?

Lesson 4: The Risk of Vulnerability

1. What do you know about vulnerable bodies? What might these bodies teach us about the church body? How do these bodies elicit a deeper embrace of each other?

2. Take a moment to write down one need you currently have. Who will you speak that need to? Does speaking that need feel like a risk? Why or why not?

3. Make a list of the groups or organizations you'd consider yourself to be a member of. What do they have in common? How is membership in the local church distinct? Why have you joined or not joined a local church?

Lesson 5: The Edge of Discernment

1. When have you lost yourself in a relationship? How did you regain your edge—that boundary between the individual self and the communal one?

2. When discerning whether to belong to a church, Erin wants to feel as if her gifts are both needed and valued. How have you discerned the balance between choosing a faith community in which you are both stretched and nurtured?

3. A healthy community is a realistic community. What one practice, if done faithfully by your church, would allow you to be real in that setting and help others to do the same?

Lesson 6: Offering My Portion

1. Do you need the church? How do you think the church needs you and your gifts in particular?

2. What is your vision of the kingdom come? Who have you tested your vision with? How will you begin to make your vision a reality?

3. What helps you hold the tension of longing and belonging? What signs are there that your belonging is already settled? What signs are there that your longing is leading you home?

NOTES

Preface: The Gift of Disillusionment

[1]Sheldon Vanauken, *A Severe Mercy: Davy's Edition* (San Francisco: Harper & Row, 1977), p. 33.

[2]Parker J. Palmer, *The Promise of Paradox: A Celebration of Contradictions in the Christian Life* (San Francisco: Jossey-Bass, 2008), p. 34.

[3]When the disciples asked Jesus what it meant to be "made free," he answered, "Very truly, I tell you, everyone who commits sin is a slave to sin. The slave does not have a permanent place in the household; the son has a place there forever. So if the Son makes you free, you will be free indeed" (John 8:34-36).

[4]Pew Forum on Religion & Public Life, "'Nones' on the Rise," October 9, 2012, www.pewforum.org/2012/10/09/nones-on-the-rise/.

[5]Ibid.

[6]Lydia Saad, "In U.S., Rise in Religious 'Nones' Slows in 2012," Gallup, January 10, 2013, www.gallup.com/poll/159785/rise-religious-nones -slows-2012.aspx#1.

[7]Pew Forum, "'Nones' on the Rise."

[8]Palmer, *The Promise of Paradox*, p. 18.

[9]Ibid., p. xxxiii.

Lesson 1: The Importance of Being Earnest

[1]Brené Brown, *Daring Greatly: How the Courage to be Vulnerable Transforms the Way We Live, Love, Parent and Lead* (New York: Gotham, 2012), p. 232.

[2]Brené Brown, *The Gifts of Imperfection: Let Go of Who You Think You're Supposed to Be and Embrace Who You Are* (Center City, MN: Hazelden, 2010), p. 26.

[3]Brian Hiatt, "Mumford & Sons: Rattle and Strum," *Rolling Stone*, March 28, 2013, www.rollingstone.com/music/news/mumford-sons-rattle-and-strum -20130328.

[4]Lillian Daniel, *When "Spiritual but Not Religious" Is Not Enough: Seeing God in Surprising Places, Even the Church* (New York: Jericho Books, 2013), p. 13.

[5]Emily Enders Odom, "Stated Clerk releases PC(USA) 2012 statistics," May 30, 2013, www.pcusa.org/news/2013/5/30/stated-clerk-releases-pcusa -2012-statistics/.

[6]W. E. Vine, "Earnest," in *Vine's Expository Dictionary of New Testament Words*, accessed May 31, 2014, www.blueletterbible.org/lang/lexicon/lexicon .cfm?Strongs=G603.

[7]W. H. Murray, *The Scottish Himalayan Expedition* (London: J. M. Dent & Sons, 1951), p. 7.

[8]For self-assessment junkies, see Laurie Beth Jones, *The Four Elements of Success: A Simple Personality Profile That Will Transform Your Team* (Nashville: Thomas Nelson, 2006).

[9]Cynthia Bourgeault, *The Holy Trinity and the Law of Three: Discovering the Radical Truth at the Heart of Christianity* (Boston: Shambhala, 2013), p. 98.

[10]Matt Soniak, "Do You Own Space Above Your House?" Mental Floss, June 25, 2012, mentalfloss.com/article/31018/do-you-own-space-above-your-house.

Lesson 2: The Art of Reading Charitably

[1]Jim Wallis, "The Post-Cynical Christian," *Sojourners*, June 20, 2013, http:// sojo.net/blogs/2013/06/20/post-cynical-christian.

[2]Tim and Kathy Keller, *The Meaning of Marriage: Facing the Complexities of Commitment with the Wisdom of God* (New York: Dutton, 2011), p. 22.

[3]Joel Stein, "Millennials: The Me Me Me Generation," *Time*, May 20, 2013.

[4]Jeffrey Jensen Arnett, *Emerging Adulthood: The Winding Road from Late Teens Through the Twenties* (New York: Oxford University Press, 2004), p. 312.

[5]Jennifer M. Silva, "Young and Isolated," *New York Times*, June 22, 2013, http://opinionator.blogs.nytimes.com/2013/06/22/young-and-isolated/?_r=0.

[6]Ibid.

[7]Gallup Poll, "Confidence in Institutions," June 1-4, 2013, www.gallup.com /poll/1597/confidence-institutions.aspx.

[8]Keller, *The Meaning of Marriage*, p. 29.

[9]W. E. Vine, "Unity," in *Vine's Expository Dictionary of New Testament Words*, accessed March 1, 2014, www.blueletterbible.org/search/Dictionary /viewTopic.cfm?topic=VT0003146.

[10]Eric Mount Jr., *Covenant, Community, and the Common Good: An Interpretation of Christian Ethics* (Cleveland: Pilgrim Press, 1999), p. 24.

[11]Mandy Aftel, *Essence & Alchemy: A Natural History of Perfume* (New York: North Pointe Press, 2001), pp. 20-21.

[12]John O'Donohue, *Eternal Echoes: Exploring Our Yearning to Belong* (New York: Cliff Street Books, 1999), p. 159.

[13]Keller, *The Meaning of Marriage*, p. 125.

[14]Dorothy Sayers, *Are Women Human?* (Grand Rapids: Eerdmans, 1971), p. 33.

[15]See Anne Fausto-Sterling's *Sexing the Body: Gender Politics and the Construction of Sexuality* (New York: Basic Books, 2000) to read about how the binary model of sex is an inaccurate account of reality. If there are more than two categories of sex found in nature, it would follow that there could be more than two possible expressions of gender behavior.

[16]Keller, *The Meaning of Marriage*, p. 65.

[17]Barbara Brown Taylor, "Sacramental Sky" (sermon, Duke University, Durham, NC, February 28, 2010), www.youtube.com/watch?v=XMrGK1JG4GA.

[18]Keller, *The Meaning of Marriage*, p. 182.

[19]Marguerite Shuster, "The Triune God," in *Exploring & Proclaiming the Apostles' Creed*, ed. Roger E. Van Harm (Grand Rapids: Eerdmans, 2004), p. 7.

[20]Tertullian, *De cultu feminarum*, section 1:1, part 2.

Lesson 3: The Discipline of Showing Up

[1]Fred R. Shapiro, *The Yale Book of Quotations* (New Haven, CT: Yale University Press, 2006), p. 17.

[2]Erwin Fahlbusch et al., eds., *The Encyclopedia of Christianity*, vol. 2 (Grand Rapids: Eerdmans, 2001), p. 173.

[3]Pope St. Pius X, "On Frequent and Daily Reception of Holy Communion," December 20, 1905, www.ewtn.com/library/CURIA/CDWFREQ.HTM.

[4]James F. White, *The Sacraments in Protestant Practice and Faith* (Nashville: Abingdon Press, 1999), pp. 86-87.

[5]Frank Thistle, "The Swingingest Sexpot in Show Business," *Adam* 7, no. 4 (1963).

[6]Alexander Schmemann, *For the Life of the World* (Crestwood, NY: St. Vladimir's Seminary Press, 1973), p. 27.

[7]Parker J. Palmer, *The Company of Strangers: Christians and the Renewal of America's Public Life* (New York: Crossroad, 1983), p. 21.

[8]Notably, the number of young black adults ages 18 to 29 going to historically black churches has remained relatively stable from 2007 to 2012. See Pew Forum, "'Nones' on the Rise," and Bryan T. Calvin, "Why Aren't Black Millennials Leaving the Church?" August, 21, 2013, www.relevantmagazine.com/god/church/why-aren%E2%80%99t-black-millennials-leaving-church.

[9]Pope Francis, "Celebration of Holy Mass" (homily, July 8, 2013), www
.vatican.va/holy_father/francesco/homilies/2013/documents/papa-francesco
_20130708_omelia-lampedusa_en.html.

[10]See David Kinnaman's *You Lost Me: Why Young Christians Are Leaving
Church and Rethinking Faith* (Grand Rapids: Baker Books, 2011).

[11]Flannery O'Connor, *Mystery and Manners: Occasional Prose*, ed. Sally and
Robert Fitzgerald (New York: Farrar, Straus & Giroux, 1969), p. 132.

[12]Rubie S. Watson, "The Named and the Nameless: Gender and Person in
Chinese Society," *American Ethnologist* 13:4 (1986): 619.

[13]Barbara Bodenhorn and Gabriele vom Bruck, eds., *An Anthropology of
Names and Naming* (New York: Cambridge University Press, 2006), p. 5.

[14]Janet Martin Soskice, *The Kindness of God: Metaphor, Gender, and Religious
Language* (New York: Oxford University Press, 2008), p. 83.

[15]Clement of Alexandria, "Miscellanies 5, xii, 78-82," in *Documents in Early
Christian Thought*, ed. Maurice Wiles and Mark Santer (Cambridge, UK:
Cambridge University Press, 1975), p. 7.

[16]Emily Dickinson, "Tell all the truth but tell it slant," in *The Poems of Emily
Dickinson: Reading Edition*, ed. Ralph W. Franklin (Cambridge, MA:
Belknap Press, 2005), p. 494.

[17]William Stafford, *The Way It Is: New and Selected Poems* (Minneapolis:
Graywolf Press, 1998), p. 165.

[18]E. B. White, "The Art of the Essay No. 1," interview by George Plimpton
and Frank H. Crowther, *The Paris Review*, no. 48 (1969).

Lesson 4: The Risk of Vulnerability

[1]According to the *Catechism of the Catholic Church*, 2nd ed., only people born
into the Protestant faith can validly practice it (818).

[2]John Calvin, *Ioannis Calvini Institutio Christianae Religionis*, trans. August
Tholuck (Charleston, SC: Nabu Press, 2010), p. 222.

[3]James R. Edwards, ed., *The Gospel According to Mark*, The Pillar New
Testament Commentary Series, ed. D. A. Carson (Grand Rapids: Eerdmans,
2002), p. 163.

[4]See Candida Moss, "The Man with the Flow of Power: Porous Bodies in
Mark 5:25-34," *Journal of Biblical Literature* 129, no. 3 (2010): 507-19.

[5]Maude W. Gleason, "Elite Male Identity in the Roman Empire," in *Life,
Death, and Entertainment in the Roman Empire*, ed. D. S. Potter and D. J.
Mattingly (Ann Arbor: The University of Michigan Press, 1999), p. 71.

[6]See Judith Butler, *Precarious Life: The Powers of Mourning and Violence* (New York: Verso, 2004).

[7]Meg Wheatley, *So Far from Home: Lost and Found in Our Brave New World* (San Francisco: Berrett-Koehler Publishers, 2012), p. 53.

[8]Ibid.

[9]Susan K. Wood, "The Holy Catholic Church, the Communion of Saints," in *Exploring & Proclaiming the Apostles' Creed*, ed. Roger E. Van Harn (Grand Rapids: Eerdmans, 2004), p. 231.

[10]Alex Williams, "Friends of a Certain Age: Why Is it Hard to Make Friends Over 30?" *New York Times*, July 13, 2012, www.nytimes.com/2012/07/15/fashion/the-challenge-of-making-friends-as-an-adult.html?pagewanted=all&_r=0.

[11]Kathleen Norris, *The Cloister Walk* (New York: Riverhead Books, 1996), p. 141.

[12]David Whyte, *The House of Belonging* (Moorhead, MN: Many Rivers Press, 1997), pp. 29-33.

[13]Charles E. Lawless Jr., *Membership Matters: Insight from Effective Churches on New Membership Classes and Assimilation* (Grand Rapids: Zondervan, 2005), p. 22.

[14]Thom S. Rainer, "Seven Trends in Church New Member Classes," November 16, 2013, http://thomrainer.com/2013/11/16/seven-trends-in-church-new-member-classes/.

[15]Robert Haight, S.J., *Christian Community in History, Volume 2* (New York: Continuum, 2005), p. 54.

[16]Ibid., p. 113.

Lesson 5: The Edge of Discernment

[1]Durham Police, "2013 Annual Report," March 6, 2013, http://durhamnc.gov/ich/op/DPD/Documents/2013AnnualReport.pdf.

[2]Samuel Wells and Marcia A. Owen, *Living Without Enemies: Being Present in the Midst of Violence* (Downers Grove, IL: InterVarsity Press, 2011), p. 82.

[3]Parker J. Palmer, *A Hidden Wholeness: The Journey Toward an Undivided Life* (San Francisco: Jossey-Bass, 2004), p. 54.

[4]"Why a 'Fellowship' of Presbyterians? A Response from Within the PC(USA)," accessed July 31, 2013, www.fellowship-pres.org/why-a-fellowship/#more-2072.

[5]"Good Friday," Catholic Online, accessed November 15, 2013, www.catholic.org/clife/lent/friday.php.

[6]Pauli Murray, *Proud Shoes* (Boston: Beacon Press, 1999), p. 267.

[7]M. Scott Peck, *The Different Drum: Community Making and Peace* (New York: Touchstone, 1987), p. 65.

[8]Fred Bahnson, *Soil and Sacrament: A Spiritual Memoir of Food and Faith* (New York: Simon and Schuster, 2013), p. 116.

Lesson 6: Offering My Portion

[1]Tara Woodard-Lehman, "Do You Really Need the Church?" *Huffington Post*, August 14, 2013, www.huffingtonpost.com/tara-woodardlehman/do-you-really-need-church_b_3751147.html.

[2]Tertullian, "On Baptism 1-9," in *Documents in Early Christian Thought*, ed. Maurice Wiles and Mark Santer (Cambridge, UK: Cambridge University Press, 2005), p. 174.

[3]As quoted in Cathleen Falsani, "There's Something in the Air: Grace," August 1, 2013, http://cathleenfalsani.religionnews.com/2013/08/01/theres -something-in-the-air-grace/.

[4]Frederick Buechner, *Telling Secrets* (New York: HarperCollins, 1991), p. 30.

[5]Roy M. Oswald and Barry Johnson, *Managing Polarities in Congregations: Eight Keys for Thriving Faith Communities* (Herndon, VA: The Alban Institute, 2010), p. 187.

[6]Thomas Gates, *Members of One Another: The Dynamics of Membership in Quaker Meeting* (Wallingford, PA: Pendle Hill Publications, 2004), p. 5.

[7]W. E. Vine, "Belong," in *Vine's Expository Dictionary of New Testament Words*, accessed March 1, 2014, www.blueletterbible.org/search/Dictionary /viewTopic.cfm?topic=VT0000262.

[8]J. Conrad, "מָנָה," in *Theological Dictionary of the Old Testament*, ed. G. J. Botterweck, Helmer Ringgren and Heinz-Josef Fabry, trans. Douglas W. Stott, 8 vols. (Grand Rapids: Eerdmans, 1984), pp. 396-401.

[9]I. Howard Marshall, "The Gospel of Luke: A Commentary on the Greek Text," in *The New International Greek Testament Commentary* (Grand Rapids: Eerdmans, 1978), p. 172.

[10]Marshall Sahlins, "The Spirit of the Gift," in *Stone Age Economics* (New York: Aldine de Gruter, 1972), p. 182.

[11]John O'Donohue, *Eternal Echoes: Exploring Our Yearning to Belong* (New York: Cliff Street Books, 1999), p. 249.

[12]Dori Baker, "Worried About the Church? Meet These Young Christian Leaders," *Faith and Leadership*, August 27, 2013, www.faithandleadership.com/content /dori-baker-worried-about-the-church-meet-these-young-christian-leaders.

[13]Chaeyoon Lim, Carol Ann MacGregor and Robert D. Putnam, "Secular and Liminal: Discovering Heterogeneity Among Religious Nones," *Journal for the Scientific Study of Religion* 49, no. 4 (2010): 609.

[14]Robert P. Jones, "Don't Write off Mainline Protestants," *Faith and Leadership*, February 26, 2013, www.faithandleadership.com/qa/robert-p-jones -dont-write-mainline-protestants.

[15]Adam Kahane, *Solving Tough Problems: An Open Way of Talking, Listening, and Creating New Realities* (San Francisco: Berrett-Koehler, 2004), pp. 83-84.

[16]Parker J. Palmer, *Healing the Heart of Democracy: The Courage to Create a Politics Worthy of the Human Spirit* (San Francisco: Jossey-Bass, 2011), pp. 60-61.

IVP *Crescendo*
COURAGE. CONFIDENCE. CALLING.

Some voices challenge us. Others support or encourage us. Voices can move us to change our minds, draw close to God, discover a new spiritual gift. The voices of others are shaping who we are.

The voices behind IVP Crescendo join together to draw us into God's story. We'll discover God's work around the globe even as we learn to love the people around the corner. We'll have opportunity to heal our places of pain. We'll discover new ways to love our families. We'll hear God's voice speaking into our lives as we discover new places of influence.

IVP Crescendo invites you to join in the rising chorus

- *to listen to the voices of others*
- *to hear the voice of God*
- *and to grow your own voice in*

COURAGE. CONFIDENCE. CALLING.

ivpress.com/crescendo
ivpress.com/crescendo-social